WITNESS LEE

The BASIC REVELATION *in the* HOLY SCRIPTURES

Living Stream Ministry
Anaheim, CA • www.lsm.org

First Edition, December 1984.

Library of Congress Catalog
Card Number: 84-52737

ISBN 978-0-87083-105-8

Published by

Living Stream Ministry
2431 W. La Palma Ave., Anaheim, CA 92801 U.S.A.
P. O. Box 2121, Anaheim, CA 92814 U.S.A.

Printed by CPI Group (UK) Ltd, Croydon CR0 4YY

14   15   16   17   18   19   /   12   11   10   9   8   7

CONTENTS

FOREWORD

The chapters in this book are taken from messages given by Witness Lee in Irving, Texas in the fall of 1983. They cover the basic and fundamental revelation contained in the Word of God. The Bible as the complete divine revelation is profound, and although it reveals many truths, its essential revelation is embodied in seven. They are God's plan, Christ's redemption, the Spirit's application, the believers, the church, the kingdom, and the New Jerusalem.

God's plan includes His good pleasure, His purpose, and His divine economy with His selection, predestination, and creation of man. All that God planned was accomplished through Christ's redemption. For the accomplishment of redemption Christ took four major steps—incarnation, crucifixion, resurrection, and ascension. The all-inclusive, life-giving Spirit applies all that the Father planned and everything the Son accomplished to the believers who are the components of the church, which is God's goal. The kingdom is the sphere or realm where God carries out His purpose, accomplishes His will, exercises His justice, displays His multifarious wisdom, and rules in His life. The New Jerusalem is the conclusion of God's entire revelation in His economy. It is the ultimate consummation of God's building work through all the generations.

Those of us who were in the meetings when these messages were given can never forget the depth of the revelation that was poured forth. Many of us felt that for the first time we had truly seen the essence of the divine revelation. The vision concerning all these precious truths was deeply wrought into us as the Word was being opened. This is a word that all the Lord's children need to hear, and we pray that the contents of this book will be a timely word for many. We worship the Lord that He has spoken such an all-embracing word through our brother and that it could be made available to all at this time. We need to pray and fellowship over all the verses and matters contained in the following chapters, looking to the Lord to grant us a clear vision concerning the basic revelation in the holy Scriptures. May the Lord grant each of us a spirit of wisdom and revelation in the full knowledge of all these truths, and may we experientially enter into the reality of each one. We also pray that these messages will bear much fruit throughout the earth.

December, 1984   Benson Phillips
    Irving, Texas

CHAPTER ONE

GOD'S PLAN

Scripture Reading: Eph. 1:4-5, 9-11; 3:2, 8-9, 11; Col. 1:25; 1 Cor. 9:17; 1 Pet. 1:1-2; Rom. 8:30; Gen. 1:26a, 27; 2:7; Zech. 12:1

The divine revelation in the sixty-six books of the Bible is exceedingly profound. There are seven basic points to this profound revelation. The first three points are God's plan, Christ's redemption, and the Spirit's application. These three points involve the Divine Trinity—God, Christ, and the Spirit. What God planned, He has accomplished through Christ's redemption. What He has accomplished in Christ, He applies to us by the Spirit. The last four points are the believers, the church, the kingdom, and the ultimate consummation—the New Jerusalem. In this chapter we will cover the first item of the basic revelation in the Bible—God's plan.

GOD'S GOOD PLEASURE—HIS HEART'S DESIRE

The Bible clearly reveals God's plan. Most Christians treasure two books among Paul's writings—Romans and Ephesians. Romans begins with our condition as sinners, fallen mankind, but Ephesians opens by bringing us into God's heart. In Romans 1 we can see our condition as sinners, but in Ephesians 1 we can see that there is something in the heart of God. The phrase *good pleasure* is used twice in this chapter (vv. 5, 9). God has a good pleasure, and this good pleasure is His heart's desire. In eternity past God was alone. We cannot imagine what it was like in that past eternity, but Ephesians 1 tells us that before the creation of the universe God had a heart's desire. He had a good pleasure. What He wanted can be expressed by the single word *sonship* (v. 5). Sonship is God's heart's desire.

After God made Adam, He said that it was not good for man to be alone (Gen. 2:18). This word can also be applied to God in eternity past. It was not good for God to be alone. He had a desire to bring forth many sons. Ephesians 1 tells us that God predestinated us unto sonship. Many Christians may think that God's predestination is unto salvation, but according to Ephesians, in eternity past the first thought in God's heart was not salvation. His foremost thought was sonship. God foreknew that His creation would fall. Because of the fall, there was the plan of salvation, so salvation was purposed for sonship. God's desire is to bring forth many sons.

Recently, at a prayer meeting in Irving, Texas, I saw three young men. By looking at their faces, I could see that they were the sons of a certain brother. The three of them bear a strong resemblance to their father; they are his very expression.

The more sons a father has, the more expression he has. Romans 8:29 tells us that the only begotten Son of God became the Firstborn among many brothers. God's only begotten Son in John 1:18 and 3:16 became through resurrection (Acts 13:33) the firstborn Son. *Firstborn* implies that other sons followed. Now God has not only one Son but many. The firstborn Son of God, Christ, has millions of brothers. Throughout these twenty centuries many have been regenerated and thus have become God's sons. All these sons are the brothers of the firstborn Son of God (John 20:17; Heb. 2:10-12). What a great, vast sonship!

When I was a young man, I was with some saints who knew the Bible very well. They stressed God's predestination, but I never heard them say what the goal of God's predestination is. After many years of studying the Bible, I saw that we were predestinated unto sonship. Subconsciously, I thought that we were predestinated unto salvation. Some would say that we were predestinated unto heaven. It is neither salvation nor heaven that is the goal of God's predestination; it is sonship (Eph. 1:5).

The King James Version translates this word as "the adoption of children," but the word in the original language means "sonship." It does not mean children adopted by a father but rather sons born directly of a begetting father. God's heart's desire, then, is to have a vast multitude of sons who express Him, not only in this age but for eternity.

GOD'S PURPOSE—HIS PLAN

Based upon His heart's desire, God made a purpose (3:11). God's purpose was made according to His good pleasure. Ephesians 1:9 says that God purposed His good pleasure. This means that according to what He desired, He made a plan. Since God had such a good pleasure, He made a plan. In Ephesians 3:11 Paul tells us again that God made a plan in Christ, a plan of the ages, an eternal plan, an eternal purpose.

GOD'S ECONOMY—
HIS ADMINISTRATIVE ARRANGEMENT

Economy is an anglicized word from the Greek *oikonomia*. It means "the law of a household," or "household administration." In 1 Timothy 1:4 this word is used for "arrangement," "plan," "administration," or "management." In the Old Testament Pharaoh's house was in need of some household management or arrangement, and Joseph was put into a position to take care of that management. What he did was mainly to distribute the rich food to the hungry (Gen. 41:33-41, 54-57), and that distribution was a dispensing. The management of Pharaoh's house was an economy carried out to dispense the riches to the people. In the New Testament this word is mainly used by Paul. But the same word was used by the Lord Jesus in Luke 16:2-4, referring to the stewardship of a steward. Joseph might be considered as Pharaoh's steward, and his responsibility was his stewardship. That duty, his stewardship, was to dispense the rich food that Pharaoh possessed to feed the starving.

His Dispensation

In Ephesians Paul tells us that he was appointed by God as a steward and that God gave him the responsibility, the duty, that is called the stewardship (3:2). The Greek word for *stewardship* is the same as the word for *dispensation*. Whether it is translated into "stewardship" or into "dispensation" depends upon the context. In Ephesians 3:2 Paul says that God gave him the stewardship of the grace of God. Then the same Greek word, *oikonomia,* is found in 1:10 and 3:9, where it seems better to translate it as "dispensation." This word *economy* mainly denotes a plan, an administration, a management, to dispense one's riches to others.

Paul considered that God had a big family to supply with His riches. In Ephesians 3:8 he says that God appointed him to preach, to minister, to distribute, or to dispense the unsearchable riches of Christ. These riches are for God's household. There is a store of the unsearchable riches of Christ, and God appointed the apostles (Peter, John, James, and Paul) to be stewards to dispense these riches to all God's chosen people.

Stewardship is the same as dispensing. Joseph carried out his stewardship by dispensing food. His responsibility, his office, his duty, was to distribute the rich food to the needy ones. That distribution was a dispensing.

Some Bible teachers have taught that there are seven dispensations in the Bible. In the Old Testament there are the dispensations of innocence, conscience, human government, promise, and law. Then in the New Testament there is the dispensation of grace in this age and the dispensation of the kingdom in the coming age. In these seven dispensations, they say, God deals with man in seven different ways.

This may be correct, but do not forget that the dispensations are God's household administration. God has a great family, and within this household He needs some administration, some plan, some management, for dispensing Himself into His household. God's main thought, even from eternity past, was to have an arrangement throughout the ages to dispense Himself into His chosen and predestinated people. He would make them His sons by imparting Himself into them so that they might have the divine life by being born again.

In Paul's fourteen Epistles we can see that God had a good pleasure, according to which He made a plan, a purpose. He created man in His own image, and in the fullness of time He imparted Himself into all these created and chosen ones that they might become His sons, expressing Him. This is God's plan, and this is God's dispensation for His dispensing.

In English the words *dispensation* and *dispensing* are both forms of the verb *to dispense*. When I use the word *dispensation,* I mean economy, arrangement, or management. But when I use the word *dispensing,* I mean the distributing of the divine riches into God's people. *Dispensation* denotes the arrangement, the management, the plan, the economy. *Dispensing* refers to the distribution of God Himself as life and the life supply into His chosen people in Christ.

His Dispensing

In Ephesians 1:10 and 3:9 the word *oikonomia* is used for "household administration," which is God's plan to dispense Himself into His chosen people. In Ephesians 3:2, Colossians 1:25, and 1 Corinthians 9:17, the same word refers to Paul's stewardship. The word *stewardship* is used in the sense of dispensing. Paul's stewardship was the dispensing of the unsearchable riches of Christ into God's chosen people. With Paul the word *stewardship* refers to the divine dispensing.

The word *steward* is used in 1 Peter 4:10, which says that we all need to be good stewards, dispensing the varied grace of God. The varied grace of the rich God needs many stewards to dispense it; this dispensing is their stewardship.

What I am doing in the ministry is dispensing the riches of Christ. If you tell me that I am a good Bible teacher, I appreciate your word, but I do not like to hear it. Do not consider me a teacher. I am a dispenser. I am not merely teaching the Bible; I am dispensing. I once went to get a flu shot. There was a long line of people, and all of us had to offer our arm so that we could get the shot. In my ministry I want to give people a shot, an injection, of the riches of Christ. I have the full assurance that whoever comes to this ministry will get such an injection.

Our stewardship today is the same as Paul's. Paul's stewardship was simply to give people an injection: that is, to distribute, to dispense, the unsearchable riches of Christ into God's chosen people. This is God's economy, His plan, His administration.

GOD'S SELECTION

God had a good pleasure, and according to His good pleasure,

He made a plan. Following this, He arranged a universal administration of His household to dispense His riches into His chosen people. Then He selected us, not only before we were created but also before the foundation of the world (Eph. 1:4; 1 Pet. 1:1-2). Nothing of His creation had yet come into existence when He selected us.

It is difficult to buy things in a shopping center because there are so many things to choose from. People do not buy blindly; they consider and choose carefully what they will buy. In eternity past, before His creation, God saw you and said, "I like that one." Without being selected, I do not believe I could have become a Christian. Even though I was born into Christianity, I was not a Christian until I was nineteen years of age. I was educated within Christianity, but I still did not believe. However, one day God touched me and said, "I want you." That day I was caught. How about you? Behind the scenes there is an eternal and almighty hand directing everything. Our selection is a wonderful thing.

Our heavenly Father is happy when He sees us. We are His heart's desire, His good pleasure. God's pleasure is not with the moon, the sun, the heavens, or the earth. He tells us clearly in His Word that He is not satisfied merely with the earth and the heavens. What satisfies Him is His chosen people. We are His good pleasure, and His plan was made for us.

HIS PREDESTINATION

Following His selection, God predestinated us (Eph. 1:5; Rom. 8:30). Darby's New Translation of the Bible translates this word *predestinated* in Ephesians 1:5 as "marked out beforehand." Have you ever realized that before the foundation of the world you were marked out? You cannot escape God's hand. I have tried a number of times, but I never made it! The more I tried, the stronger He grasped me. Where will you go to escape God? Wherever you go, He is there (Psa. 139:7-10). Sometimes you may have been bored with coming to the church meetings and decided to go somewhere else. When you got there, the Lord Jesus was waiting for you! This shows that you have been marked out.

GOD'S CREATION

After God's good pleasure, after His plan (arrangement, administration, economy), after His selection, and after His predestination, He came to His creation. The record of God's creation of man is very brief. There are only two verses. Genesis 1:26 is God's own word, and the following verse is Moses' record. In these two verses are three crucial points.

The Council of the Divine Trinity

First, verse 26 indicates the Divine Trinity. The word *Elohim (God)* is plural, and in God's own conversation He used the pronouns *Us* and *Our*: "Let Us make man in Our image, according to Our likeness." The pronouns referring to God are plural. It is easy to realize that this implies the Divine Trinity.

Some teachers have pointed out that when God said, "Let Us make man...," it was a conversation in a council. The Divine Trinity had a council to consider the creation of man. In creating other things there was no such conversation recorded. The making of man, then, must have been crucial. To create the heavens and the earth was not as important as the making of man. Man is the focus of God's purpose in creation.

The Creation of Man
in God's Image, according to God's Likeness

Second, only man was made in the image of God and according to God's likeness. The tiger was not made in God's image; nor was the elephant made according to His likeness. Genesis 1:26 says, "Let Us make man in Our image, according to Our likeness."

Image refers to the inward being; *likeness* refers to the outward expression. You may refer to Colossians 1:15, which speaks of Christ as "the image of the invisible God." How can an invisible God have an outward likeness? I cannot explain this. It is a mystery. It is like John 1:14, which says that God as the Word became flesh. In Genesis 18, however, He appeared to Abraham as a man. Abraham prepared water for Him to wash His feet and prepared a meal for Him (vv. 4-8).

He appeared again in Judges 13, this time to Samson's mother. She saw this man, who, after talking to her and her husband, ascended (v. 20). Here is an ascension before Acts 1. How can we reconcile these portions of the Old Testament with the New Testament? We cannot.

In the same way it is a wonder, a mystery, that God created man in His image. Second Corinthians 3:18 says that we are being transformed into His image. Romans 12:2 says that we are "transformed by the renewing of the mind." These verses indicate that the image is something inward, made up of the mind, emotion, and will. The thinking organ, the loving organ, and the deciding organ compose the inward being. Man is wonderfully made. Even after the fall, man is still marvelous (Psa. 139:14). We are marvelous beings because we were created by God in this way.

For God's Expression

Third, man was made to express God. *Image* and *likeness* both denote expression. When God created man in His image and according to His likeness, He did not put the divine life into him. The divine life was not imparted into the created man until Jesus came and died and was resurrected for us. Now everyone who believes into Him has eternal life (John 3:16). If we have the Son, we have this divine life. If we do not have the Son, we do not have this life (1 John 5:12). God's life did not enter into the created man until the accomplishment of Christ's full redemption.

Of Three Parts

God created man with the intention that one day He would enter into man and that man would be able to receive Him. Romans 9 reveals that the man created by God is a vessel, intended to contain something. Just as a cup is a vessel to hold water, so man was made as a vessel to contain God.

Genesis 2:7 tells us how God made man. He made man's body from the dust of the ground. Then He breathed the breath of life into the nostrils of this body of dust, and man became a living soul. Here in this one verse there is the body, the soul, and the breath of life. The Hebrew word for *breath* in Genesis

2:7 is translated "spirit" in Proverbs 20:27, which says, "The spirit of man is the lamp of Jehovah." This indicates that the very breath of life breathed into Adam was the human spirit. Two materials, then, were used to form man: the dust and the breath of life. The dust became the body, and the breath of life became the spirit. When these two things came together, a by-product came out: the soul. Thus, Paul tells us in 1 Thessalonians 5:23 that a human being is of three parts: spirit, soul, and body.

Genesis 1 tells us that God created man in His own image, according to His likeness; this was so that he could contain God. A container must be in the shape of the thing it will contain. If something is square, you would not make a round container for it. If something is round, you would not make a square container for it. The shape of the container is made according to the shape of its contents. Man was made in the image and likeness of God.

Genesis 1 tells us that everything created brought forth according to its kind (vv. 11-12, 21, 24-25). The apple tree brings forth according to its kind, and the tiger according to its kind. Man was made according to God's kind. If two trees are grafted together, they must be of the same kind; otherwise, the grafting will not take. Hallelujah! Man is of the same kind as God! Because we were created according to God's kind, with the intention that we would be grafted together with God, this "grafting" will take, and we can be made one with God.

The Crucial Part—Man's Spirit

God created man with a spirit, although at the time of creation he did not have God's life. Hence, the Bible says, "There is a spirit in man" (Job 32:8). Twenty-two years ago when I began to minister in this country, I gave message after message on the human spirit. Many saints told me that they had never before heard of this. Andrew Murray and Mrs. Jessie Penn-Lewis both stressed the spirit. God created us not only with a mouth and a stomach to receive physical food; He also created us with a spirit to receive Him.

Inside a radio is a receiver. Without the receiver, none of the radio waves from the air could be received by the radio.

Our receiver to receive God is our spirit. The Lord Jesus said in John 4:24, "God is Spirit, and those who worship Him must worship in spirit and truthfulness." Only spirit can worship Spirit. Because God Himself is Spirit, He created us with a spirit for the definite purpose that we might worship Him. To worship Him includes contacting Him, conversing with Him, and receiving Him. He comes into us by entering into our spirit.

Romans 8:16 says that the Spirit and our spirit witness together. This means that the Spirit of God, upon our believing in the Lord Jesus, comes into our spirit. First Corinthians 6:17 says, "He who is joined to the Lord is one spirit." At the beginning of the Bible God prepared a man in His image, according to His likeness, and with a spirit to receive, contain, and express Him. However, at the time of creation man did not receive God, the divine Spirit, into his spirit.

Every human being has God's image, God's likeness, and a human spirit. When the gospel reached us, it touched us in our conscience, which is a part of the spirit (cf. Rom. 8:16; 9:1). By that touch our spirit was made alive, and we repented. We opened our inner being to repent, to believe, and to receive the Lord Jesus; He came into us, and we were saved. Many gospel preachers ask, "Will you open up and invite Jesus to come into your heart?" There is nothing wrong with this, but in order to experience Christ as our life after being saved, we must know that He is now in our spirit (2 Tim. 4:22).

God's purpose is sonship, and sonship is accomplished by the dispensing of what God is into us as our life. This dispensing is in our spirit. John 3:6 says, "That which is born of the flesh is flesh, and that which is born of the Spirit is spirit." Here again are the two spirits. We were not regenerated in our mentality or in our body. Nicodemus thought that to be reborn was to be reborn in the physical body, but the Lord Jesus corrected him. To be reborn is to be reborn in our spirit of God the Spirit, not of our parents. Even if we could go back into our mother's womb and be born physically a hundred times, we would still be flesh. We must be born in our spirit of the divine Spirit.

Zechariah 12:1 tells us that there are three crucial things

in God's creation: the heavens, the earth, and the spirit of
man. It says that Jehovah is the One who "stretches forth the
heavens and lays the foundations of the earth and forms the
spirit of man within him." How great is our spirit! The heavens are for the earth. Without the heavens, the earth could not
have anything organic. The earth is for man, and man is for
God. For man to be for God, he needs a receiver. This receiver
is our human spirit. Praise the Lord that we are here under
God's plan and in His plan; that we have been made by Him in
His image and according to His likeness; that we have a spirit
to receive Him; and that He, as the divine Spirit, has entered
into our human spirit, making us His sons for His expression!
This is His plan.

CHAPTER TWO

CHRIST'S REDEMPTION

Scripture Reading: John 1:14; Heb. 2:14; Rom. 8:3; 2 Cor. 5:21;
John 3:14; 1 Pet. 2:24; 1 Cor. 15:3; Heb. 9:28; Rom. 6:6; Gal.
2:20; Eph. 2:15; John 12:24, 31; 19:34; 7:39; Luke 24:26; Acts
13:33; Rom. 8:29; Heb. 2:11-12; 1 Pet. 1:3; Eph. 2:6; 1 Cor.
15:45; 2 Cor. 3:17-18; John 20:22; Eph. 1:20-21; Acts 2:36; Eph.
1:22-23; Acts 2:33

God created the heavens and the earth with man as the
head and center. Then man fell. In the eyes of God, man's fall
involved the entire creation. To redeem this fallen creation
God came in the Son.

Redemption was not an afterthought. It was preordained
by God. First Peter 1:19-20 tells us that the Redeemer, Christ,
was foreknown by God before the foundation of the world. In
this verse *world* refers to the entire universe. Before the foundation of the universe, God knew that man would fall. Thus,
God preordained the Son, Christ, to be the Redeemer. We can
see from this that God's redemption was not accidental.

Furthermore, Revelation 13:8 says that the Lamb, that is,
the Redeemer, Christ, was slain "from the foundation of the
world." From the time creation came into existence, in the
eyes of God, Christ, as the Lamb ordained by God, was slain.
In our eyes Christ was crucified less than two thousand years
ago. But in God's view He was slain from the day creation came
into existence, because God foreknew that His creation would
fall.

These verses show that God's redemption was not an afterthought but rather something ordained, planned, and prepared
by God in eternity past. How we should treasure this fact
about the redemption we enjoy in Christ!

GOD INCARNATED

The first step in God's accomplishment of redemption was the incarnation. It was surely a marvelous thing for God to come into man and to be born of mankind through a virgin. Our God became a man. In creation He was the Creator. But though He created all things, He did not enter into any of the things He created. Even in creating man He only breathed the breath of life into him (Gen. 2:7). He was still outside man. His breath, according to Job 33:4, gave man life; however, He Himself did not come into man. Until the incarnation He was separate from man. But with the incarnation He personally entered into man. He was first conceived and then remained in the virgin's womb for nine months, after which He was born.

The Word Becoming Flesh

According to John 1:14, He became not only a man; He "became flesh." *Flesh* in this verse refers to man after the fall. Man in Genesis 1 and 2 had not fallen, but after Genesis 3 he had. The word *flesh,* referring to man after the fall, always bears a negative denotation. No flesh can be justified before God by works (Rom. 3:20). *Flesh* refers to fallen man, and Christ as the Son of God became a man. He became flesh.

In the Likeness of the Flesh of Sin

I do not mean that Christ became a sinner. The Bible is very careful about this matter. If the Bible contained only John 1:14, we might think that He became a sinful person. But the Bible also contains Romans 8:3, which says that God sent His Son "in the likeness of the flesh of sin." Christ became flesh, but He was only in the likeness of the flesh of sin. There was no sin in His flesh. He had only the likeness, not the sinful nature, of the flesh. Paul composed this phrase of three words: *likeness, flesh,* and *sin.* To say only "flesh of sin" would indicate sinful flesh. Praise the Lord that the Scripture adds *in the likeness,* indicating that in Christ's human nature there was no sin, even though that nature did bear the likeness, the appearance, of the flesh of sin. Moreover, Paul does not say that God sent His Son in the likeness of the flesh and stop there. He adds *of sin*. *Likeness* denotes strongly that Christ's humanity did not have sin, but still that His humanity was in some way related to sin.

In another verse, 2 Corinthians 5:21, Paul says that Christ "did not know sin." This means that He had no sin. Yet 2 Corinthians 5:21 also says that this One who had no sin was made sin by God. Our mentality cannot understand this. If the Scriptures were not written in this way, it would seem heretical to say that Christ was made sin, but Christ was made sin for us as our full Substitute. If this had not happened, we could not have been saved. "Him who did not know sin He made sin on our behalf." The One whom God made sin knew no sin.

This matter is portrayed in the Old Testament in the type of the bronze serpent, described in Numbers 21. When the children of Israel sinned against God, they were bitten by serpents and were dying. Moses looked to God for them, and God told him to make a bronze serpent and set it on a pole. Whoever looked at that bronze serpent would live, and many did (vv. 6-9).

Then in John 3 the Lord Jesus talked to Nicodemus about regeneration. Nicodemus was a Bible teacher (v. 10) and taught the Old Testament, especially the Pentateuch. "Nicodemus said to Him, How can a man be born when he is old? He cannot enter a second time into his mother's womb and be born, can he?" (v. 4). The Lord implied that if he could go back to his mother's womb and be born again, he would still be flesh: "That which is born of the flesh is flesh" (v. 6). To be reborn is not to be born a second time of the flesh but to be born of the Spirit. "That which is born of the Spirit is spirit" (v. 6).

Nicodemus wondered how these things could be. Then the Lord Jesus said to him in a rebuking tone, "You are a teacher of Israel, and you do not know these things?" (v. 10). He then referred Nicodemus to the record in Numbers 21: "As Moses lifted up the serpent in the wilderness, so must the Son of Man be lifted up, that everyone who believes into Him may have eternal life" (John 3:14-15).

This portrait clearly indicates that the bronze serpent bears only the appearance, the likeness, of the serpent but not its poisonous nature. This corresponds with Paul's word *in the likeness of the flesh of sin.*

When Christ died on the cross, He was not only a Lamb in the eyes of God but also a serpent. Both of these aspects of Christ are in John. John 1:29 refers to the Lamb of God, and John 3:14 refers to the Son of Man, Christ, lifted up like the bronze serpent in the wilderness. When Christ, our Redeemer, was on the cross, on the one hand, He was the Lamb of God to take away our sin; on the other hand, He was a serpent. The holy Word tells us that when Christ died on the cross, in the eyes of God He was like a bronze serpent. I stress this because we need to know what kind of redemption the Lord Jesus accomplished for us.

In order to accomplish a full redemption, He as the Son of God became flesh. The Word became incarnate. John, though, does not say that the Word became a man; he says, "The Word became flesh." By the time of the incarnation, *flesh* was a negative term. But we must be careful in saying this. A serpent surely is negative, but this serpent is a bronze serpent. It bears only the appearance of a serpent; it does not have its nature. Do you think that Christ had a sinful nature when He was made sin? Absolutely not! This is why Paul qualifies his word by saying, "who did not know sin." Even though He was made sin by God, He had no sin in Him, and He knew no sin. Our Lord is a wonderful Redeemer. The Bible tells us that God became a man in the likeness of fallen and sinful flesh.

Partaking of Man's Blood and Flesh

Incarnation also has a positive side. It brought God into man. It made God and man one. Nearly two thousand years ago there was a man on this earth who was a combination of God and man. Was Jesus Christ just man? Was He just God? He was both God and man. Many Bible teachers call Him the God-man. He was not merely a man of God but a God-man. He was the complete God and a perfect man.

According to the genuine revelation of the Bible, in such an incarnation neither the nature of God nor the nature of man was lost, and no third nature was produced. Christ is a God-man with both the divine nature and the human nature, each existing in Him distinctly.

Our Redeemer is a God-man. By His incarnation for the accomplishment of redemption, He, as the very God, took this step of making Himself one with man. He participated in man's blood and flesh. Hebrews 2:14 tells us, "Since therefore the children have shared in blood and flesh, He also Himself in like manner partook of the same." If He had not had man's blood, how could He have shed His blood for man's sins? Without shedding of blood there is no forgiveness of sins (9:22). As human beings, we need human blood to wash away our sins. Because our Redeemer partook of man's blood, He could shed His blood for our sins.

Still with the Father

When the Son of God became incarnate, He did not leave the Father in the heavens. Although I used to think so over fifty years ago, I gradually discovered by studying the Word that the Son and the Father cannot be separated. They are distinct but not separate. The Son Himself told us clearly that He came in the Father's name (John 5:43) and that the Father was with Him all the time (16:32). He and the Father are one (10:30; 17:22).

As Christians, we believe that there is only one God. To believe in tritheism, that there are three Gods, is a great heresy. We have only one God, yet our God is triune. He is three in His Godhead: the Father, the Son, and the Spirit. Yet He is one God. We have no way to reconcile this. However, we do know the revealed fact that our God is triune, that He is three-one.

God's plan is mainly the work of the Father, His redemption is mainly the work of the Son, and His application is mainly the work of the Spirit. The Father planned, the Son redeemed, and the Spirit applies.

The three are distinct but not separate. When the Son came, the Father came with Him. When the Spirit came, the Son and the Father came (14:17, 23). We do not believe in modalism, a heresy which says that when the Son came, the Father was over, and then when the Spirit came, the Son was over. We believe that God is three-one, the Father, the Son, and the Spirit as one God, coexisting and coinhering from eternity through eternity.

CRUCIFIED

The incarnation was wonderful, and the crucifixion was marvelous. We have no human words to explain the incarnation in full; neither can we fully explain the fact of Christ's death.

Bearing Our Sins

On the cross Christ bore our sins. Three verses are very clear regarding this: 1 Peter 2:24, 1 Corinthians 15:3, and Hebrews 9:28. These verses all say that Christ bore our sins. According to Isaiah 53:6, when Christ was on the cross, God took all our sins and put them upon this Lamb of God.

If you read the four Gospels concerning Christ's death, you will see that He was crucified from nine o'clock in the morning, the third hour (Mark 15:25), until three o'clock in the afternoon, the ninth hour (v. 33; Matt. 27:46). In the midst of these six hours there was noontime, the sixth hour (Mark 15:33). The noontime divided these six hours into two periods of three hours each. Man's persecution took place in the first three hours. Man nailed Him to the cross, mocked Him, and afflicted Him in every possible way. Then in the final three hours God came in to judge Him (Isa. 53:10). This is indicated by the darkness that came over the whole land at noontime. God put all the sins of mankind upon Him.

Made Sin for Us

In the last three hours, in the eyes of God Christ was made sin. It was then on the cross that God condemned sin in the flesh of Christ. Romans 8:3 says that God, sending His own Son in the likeness of the flesh of sin (as the bronze serpent in the form of a serpent—John 3:14), condemned sin in the flesh. Sin was condemned. Sin was judged on the cross. Not only did Christ bear our sins; He was made sin for us (2 Cor. 5:21) and was judged by God once for all.

With Our Old Man
and the Entire Old Creation

In addition, when Christ was crucified, all His believers were crucified with Him (Gal. 2:20). When He was incarnated, He took us upon Himself. He put on blood and flesh. Therefore, when He was crucified, we were crucified with Him. From God's viewpoint, before we were born, we were crucified in Christ. When Christ was crucified, not only were our sins dealt with and not only was our sin dealt with; we ourselves were crucified. Hence, Romans 6:6 says, "Our old man has been crucified with Him."

Besides this, the entire creation was also crucified there. When Christ died, the veil of the temple was split in two from top to bottom (Matt. 27:51). *From top to bottom* indicates that it was not man's doing but God's doing from above. God split that veil into two pieces. On the veil there were cherubim embroidered (Exo. 26:31). According to Ezekiel 1:5 and 10 and 10:14-15, cherubim were living creatures. The cherubim on the veil, then, indicated the living creatures. Upon the humanity of Christ were all the creatures. When the veil was split in two, all the creatures were crucified. By this we can see that the death of Christ was all-inclusive. It dealt with our sins, with our sin, with our self, our old man, and with the entire old creation. Sins, sin, man, and the entire creation were all dealt with on the cross.

Abolishing the Law
of the Commandments in Ordinances

In Ephesians 2:15 Paul tells us that through His death on the cross, Christ abolished the law of the commandments in ordinances. In the Old Testament there were many ordinances. The main one was circumcision, which divided the Jews from the Gentiles. The Jews even used the term *uncircumcision* in referring to the Gentiles, whereas they considered themselves the circumcision. Circumcision was, therefore, a mark of separation. The Jews also kept the seventh day, another ordinance that made them different from the Gentiles. Christ abolished both of these ordinances on the cross (Col. 2:14, 16).

Other ordinances of the Jews were the dietary regulations. In Acts 10, however, while Peter was praying on the housetop, a vision came to him (vv. 9-16). The Lord told Peter to eat the animals that he considered common and unclean. Thus, circumcision, the Sabbath, and the dietary regulations were all abolished. These ordinances had been a strong and high wall of separation between the Jews and the Gentiles, but now it was torn down. There is no longer any separation. The Jews and the Gentiles can be built together as the Body of Christ.

The ordinances have been abolished, but what about the differences between the races, such as the difference between blacks and whites? In Christ's complete redemption all these differences have also been abolished. He has done away with all the enmity. Yet many do not live according to this. The Jews still keep circumcision, the Sabbath, and the dietary regulations. Even many Christians still have enmity.

Through His one death Christ took away our sins and sin, He crucified the old man, He terminated the old creation, and He abolished the differences between the races. Now we are not in ourselves—we are in Christ. In Him there are no sins. In Him there is no sin. In Him there is no old man and no old creation. The church is simply Christ (1 Cor. 12:12). The very content, the constituent, of the church is Christ (Col. 3:10-11). In the new man there is no Greek and no Jew, no social rank, no racial distinctions, no national differences; Christ is all and in all (v. 11). In Christ sins, sin, the old man, the old creation, and all the ordinances are done away.

Destroying Satan and Judging the World

The flesh was crucified with Christ. Because the flesh is related to Satan, in crucifying the flesh Christ destroyed Satan. This is why Hebrews 2:14 says that through His death He destroyed the devil. From John 12:31 we know that when Christ was crucified, He cast out Satan, the ruler of the world, and He judged the world.

Around 1935 I heard a message given by Brother Watchman Nee in Shanghai. He said that if you went to a young believer and asked him who died on the cross, he would say that his Redeemer had died on the cross for both his sins and his sin. If

you went to another one who was more advanced and asked
him who had died on the cross, he would say that Christ died
there, bearing his sins, sin, and himself (Gal. 2:20). Someone
still more advanced in the Christian life would tell you that
Christ died on the cross for his sins, sin, and himself with all of
creation. A fourth category of Christians would say that Christ
died on the cross not only for their sins, sin, and themselves
with all of creation but also in order to destroy Satan and judge
the world.

Later, I began to see that there was the need for further
advancement in realizing the death of Christ, that is, the
abolishing of the ordinances. All the ordinances—the habits,
customs, traditions, and practices among the human race—
were abolished on the cross. Christ's crucifixion was the universal termination of all negative things. Hallelujah for such a
termination!

Releasing the Divine Life

Christ's death was not only a terminating but also a releasing death. His death released the divine life concealed within
Him (John 1:4). John 12:24 says that a grain of wheat remains
alone unless it is sown into the earth. If it is sown into the
earth, it dies and then grows up to become many grains. This
illustrates the releasing death of Christ. His death not only ter-
minates all negative things; it also releases the divine life—
the unique positive thing in the whole universe.

When Christ died, a soldier pierced His side and out came
blood and water (19:34). These are symbols. Blood signifies
redemption, and water signifies life. Blood and water are symbols of the two aspects of Christ's death. The negative aspect is
redemption, and the positive aspect is the release of the divine
life. He died, and the life within Him was released. Through His
death not only did the redeeming blood flow out; the divine life
also flowed out from Him. Today when we believe in Him, we
receive the blood and obtain the living water, the divine life.
We receive redemption, and we obtain eternal life.

RESURRECTED

On the third day after His death, Christ resurrected. Some

wonderful things have been carried out through His resurrection.

Glorified in the Divine Life

First, in His resurrection Christ was glorified. When a carnation seed is sown, it dies under the earth, and then it grows up. When it blossoms, that blossoming is its glorification. Jesus was the unique seed of the divine life. Before His death the divine life was concealed within Him. His humanity was the shell. When His humanity was broken on the cross, the divine life came out from within Him, and He was glorified in that life (7:39; Luke 24:26). Christ's entering into resurrection was like the blossoming of the carnation seed: He was glorified.

Becoming the Firstborn Son of God
with Many Brothers

Second, in resurrection Christ was born as the firstborn Son of God. Not many Christians realize that to Jesus Christ resurrection was a birth. Incarnation was His birth as a man, but resurrection was His birth in His humanity as the firstborn Son of God (Acts 13:33).

Christ as the Son of God has two aspects. Before His resurrection He was the only begotten Son (John 1:14; 3:16); then in resurrection He was born of God as the firstborn Son. When Christ was incarnated, He put on humanity; however, His humanity was not divine. It was through death and resurrection that His humanity was brought into divinity. Thus, Acts 13:33 tells us that in His resurrection He was born. The only begotten Son became the firstborn Son (Rom. 8:29).

Ephesians 2:6 tells us that in Christ's resurrection we, His believers, were also resurrected. When He was crucified, we were crucified. When He was resurrected, we were resurrected. In His resurrection He was born as the firstborn Son of God, and we also were born as the many sons of God. He became the Firstborn, and we became His many brothers (John 20:17; Heb. 2:11-12).

The Bible makes clear that before we were born, we were crucified with Christ and resurrected with Him. In resurrection He was born as the firstborn Son of God, and in His resurrection we also were born as the many sons of God (1 Pet. 1:3). He became the Firstborn among us, His many brothers.

Becoming the Life-giving Spirit

In resurrection Christ also became a life-giving Spirit (1 Cor. 15:45). This verse in 1 Corinthians is one of the most neglected verses in the Bible. In resurrection, the subject of 1 Corinthians 15, Christ as the last Adam, through His death and resurrection, became a life-giving Spirit. Many Christians consider Christ as their Redeemer, but very few consider Him as a life-giving Spirit. Our Redeemer is the life-giving Spirit in resurrection. By His death He redeemed us; in His resurrection He imparts Himself into us as life.

After His resurrection and in His resurrection, He became the pneumatic Christ. The pneumatic Christ is identical to the Spirit. This is why 2 Corinthians 3:17 says, "The Lord is the Spirit." Today in resurrection the very Christ, our Redeemer, is identical to the Spirit who gives life to us.

Breathing into His Believers

John 20 reveals that after His death and in His resurrection Christ came back. He returned in a wonderful way. The disciples were in a house with the doors shut for fear of the Jews (v. 19). Suddenly, Jesus was standing there and saying to them, "Peace be to you" (v. 21). He did not teach them, and He did not give them a sermon as He did on the mount. He simply breathed into them and said to them, "Receive the Holy Spirit" (v. 22), the Holy Breath, the Holy Pneuma.

Christ appeared without knocking at the door because in resurrection He is the Spirit. He had a resurrected body, which is called a spiritual body (1 Cor. 15:44; John 20:27). We cannot explain this, but it is a fact revealed in the Bible. From the time of His resurrection, Christ never left the believers. Here and there He appeared to them, but He was always with them.

Consider, then, what is included in His resurrection: He was glorified; He became the firstborn Son of God, making all of us His brothers; and He became the life-giving Spirit breathed into us to be with us forever (14:16-20).

EXALTED

After His resurrection, in His ascension Christ was highly exalted (Eph. 1:20-21). He was made Lord and Christ (Acts 2:36), and He was given to be the Head over all things to the church, which is His Body (Eph. 1:22-23). Our Head, Christ, is not only our Head but the Head over all things to us.

In His ascension Christ poured out the Holy Spirit upon all His believers (Acts 2:33). This was the genuine baptism of the Spirit that formed the Body of Christ (1 Cor. 12:13). In His resurrection He breathed the Holy Spirit *into* His disciples; then in His ascension He poured out His Spirit *upon* His believers. This means that within the believers and upon them there was only the Spirit. Within was the Spirit, and without was the Spirit. Within was the infilling Spirit, and without was the outpoured Spirit. This was accomplished once for all and is an eternal fact in which we participate.

Incarnation is a fact, and crucifixion is a fact, including all the accomplishments of the Lord on the cross. Resurrection is also a fact. In His resurrection Christ became the Firstborn, making us all His brothers, and He also became the life-giving Spirit breathed into us. Furthermore, the ascension is a fact. In His ascension Christ was made the Head over all things, He was made Lord and Christ, and He poured Himself out as the Spirit upon us all. Now we are in Him. He is in the heavenlies, and so are we (Eph. 2:6). He is within us and upon us, and we are in Him. This is the complete redemption of Christ.

CHAPTER THREE

THE SPIRIT'S APPLICATION

Scripture Reading: Gen. 1:2; Judg. 3:10; Luke 1:35; John 7:39; Acts 16:6-7; Rom. 8:2, 9; Phil. 1:19; 1 Cor. 15:45; 2 Cor. 3:6, 17-18; Rev. 1:4; 4:5; 5:6; 2:7; 14:13; 22:17; John 14:17; 15:26; 16:13-15; 1 John 5:6; John 3:5-6; 2 Cor. 1:21-22; Eph. 1:13; 4:30; 1 Pet. 1:2; Rom. 15:16; 1 Cor. 12:13

Prayer: Lord, how we thank You for Your word. We thank You for this gathering. We believe that it is sovereign of You. Lord, we can come to You around Your word. What a mercy and grace! We trust in You for the understanding of Your word. We admit our inadequacy. We are short—short of understanding, short of utterance, even short in listening. Anoint our ears and our minds. Anoint the speaking mouth. May You speak in our speaking. We like to practice the one spirit with You, especially in this hour in speaking Your word. Lord, do cleanse us with Your precious blood. How we thank You that where the blood is, there the rich anointing is. We trust in Your anointing. We look to You desperately for such a mysterious word tonight. Lord, defeat the enemy and chase away all the darkness from this hall. Visit every attendant. In Your mighty name we ask. Amen.

We have covered the first two items of the basic revelation in the Holy Scriptures—God's plan and Christ's redemption. In this chapter we come to the third item—the Spirit's application. This is the most mysterious item in the divine revelation.

Printing may be used as an illustration of the application of the Spirit. In printing there is first the draft, the manuscript. This manuscript is then typeset onto a page, which is then made into a negative. Then the printing press, using the negative, produces however many copies are wanted. This last stage, producing the copies, illustrates the Spirit's application.

Christ did a great work of "typesetting" what God purposed in His plan. He became incarnated and lived on earth for thirty-three and a half years. Then He died on the cross, was resurrected, and ascended to the heavens. By such a long process, from incarnation to ascension, the Lord Jesus has done the wonderful typesetting work. This work produced a "negative." Now the Spirit comes and applies to us what Christ has done. The Father planned, the Son accomplished, and the Spirit comes to apply what Christ accomplished according to the Father's plan.

For the best printing results, clean, pure paper must be used. This is why the first thing that the Spirit applies to us is the cleansing of the precious blood of the Lord Jesus (Heb. 9:14). The Spirit cleanses us with the redeeming blood of Christ. Through the precious blood we have been washed and cleansed. Now we are clean, pure paper, good for this spiritual printing.

THE SPIRIT THROUGHOUT THE WORD

To understand the Spirit's work in applying Christ's accomplishments, let us consider how the Spirit is gradually revealed throughout the Scriptures.

The Spirit of God

The first time the Spirit of God is mentioned is in Genesis 1:2. This is God the Spirit in His creation. The Spirit of God brooded over the death waters for God's creation.

The Spirit of Jehovah

After creating man, God remained intimately involved with him. In His relationship with man God's title is *Jehovah*. This is why in the Old Testament the Spirit of God is usually called the Spirit of Jehovah. The Spirit of Jehovah came upon certain people. This indicates that the Spirit of Jehovah has to do with God's reaching of man (Judg. 3:10; Ezek. 11:5). The main titles used for the Spirit of God in the Old Testament are *the Spirit of God* and *the Spirit of Jehovah*.

The Holy Spirit

At the incarnation the Spirit of God was called the Holy Spirit (Matt. 1:18, 20; Luke 1:35). In his masterpiece *The Spirit of Christ,* Andrew Murray points out that the divine title *the Holy Spirit* is not used in the Old Testament. In Psalm 51:11 and in Isaiah 63:10-11 *Holy Spirit* (KJV) should be translated as "Spirit of holiness." It was when the time came to prepare the way for Christ's coming and to prepare a human body for Him to initiate the New Testament dispensation that the term *the Holy Spirit* came into use (Luke 1:15, 35).

The Spirit Being Not Yet

Now we come to a very hard point. In John 7:37-38 the Lord Jesus cried, "If anyone thirsts, let him come to Me and drink. He who believes into Me, as the Scripture said, out of his innermost being shall flow rivers of living water." Then in verse 39 John explains that the Lord spoke this "concerning the Spirit, whom those who believed into Him were about to receive; for the Spirit was not yet, because Jesus had not yet been glorified." John does not say "the Spirit of God," "the Spirit of Jehovah," or "the Holy Spirit," but "the Spirit." He further says that when Jesus was crying out to the people, "the Spirit was not yet." The King James Version says that the Spirit "was not yet *given,*" but the word *given* is inserted; it is not in the Greek text. The Spirit of God was in Genesis 1, and the Spirit of Jehovah came upon the prophets in the Old Testament. Why, then, in John 7 was the Spirit "not yet"?

In *The Spirit of Christ* Andrew Murray indicates that before Christ's glorification, that is, before His resurrection (Luke 24:26), the Spirit of God had only divinity. But when Christ was resurrected, the Spirit of God became the Spirit of the glorified Jesus. If He were still only the Spirit of God, He would have only the divine element. Murray's word implies that the Spirit, in becoming the Spirit of the glorified Jesus following Christ's resurrection, now has the element of humanity.

The Compound Spirit

When I was young, I was taught that in Exodus 30:22-30

the anointing ointment is a type of the Holy Spirit. But after I received enlightenment through Andrew Murray's book, I went back to study Exodus 30. This ointment was composed of olive oil compounded with four spices: myrrh, cinnamon, calamus, and cassia. The olive oil is a type of the Holy Spirit, but what are the four spices? It is well known that myrrh refers to Christ's death. Cinnamon should indicate the sweet effectiveness of that death. Calamus is a reed that grows in muddy ground and shoots high into the air. This indicates resurrection. Cassia was used in ancient times as a repellent for insects and especially for snakes. This should indicate the power of Christ's resurrection that prevails against Satan.

These four spices were of three units. There were five hundred shekels of myrrh, two hundred fifty shekels each of cinnamon and calamus, and five hundred shekels of cassia. If the lamb is a type of Christ and if the olive oil is a type of the Holy Spirit, surely these four spices are also types concerning Christ. The three units of five hundred shekels each should refer to the Trinity. The total quantity of the cinnamon and calamus, being split into two half units of two hundred fifty each, typifies the second of the Trinity "split" on the cross, just as the veil was split in two from top to bottom.

The number one of the one hin of olive oil signifies the unique God. The number four of the four spices signifies the creature. In Ezekiel and in Revelation there are the four living creatures, referring to God's creation (Ezek. 1:10; Rev. 4:6-9).

By all these we can realize that this compound ointment should be an all-inclusive type of the compound Spirit referred to in John 7:39. This means that the Spirit of God, as the basic element, has been compounded with Christ's deity, humanity, death, and resurrection as the spices. In this compound Spirit are the unique God, the Trinity, man, the creature, Christ's death, the sweetness and effectiveness of His death, Christ's resurrection, and the power of His resurrection.

The Spirit was first the Spirit of God, possessing only the divine essence. But after God in the Son became a man and died on the cross, passing through death and resurrection and entering into ascension, the Spirit became the Spirit of Jesus

Christ (Phil. 1:19), compounded with God's essence and Jesus' humanity and His death and resurrection. The Spirit no longer has just the divine essence, but now has, in addition, Jesus' humanity with the death of Christ, the effectiveness of His death, the resurrection, and the power of His resurrection.

From the inner-life writings I received help to know that I was crucified before I was born (Gal. 2:20). In God's view we were crucified before we were born. As God's chosen ones, we were born crucified. Mrs. Jessie Penn-Lewis said that every Christian must die to live (John 12:24; 1 Cor. 15:31; 2 Cor. 4:11). But my experience was that the more I tried to die, the more alive I was. A hymn written by A. B. Simpson says that there is a little word that the Lord has given—*reckon*. According to Romans 6:11, we must reckon ourselves dead. I practiced reckoning, but it did not work. The more I reckoned myself dead, the more alive I seemed. In Watchman Nee's book *The Normal Christian Life* there is a chapter that stresses reckoning. That book was a compilation of messages that Brother Nee gave before 1939. After 1939 he began to tell people that we cannot experience Christ's death revealed in Romans 6 until we have the experience of the Spirit of Christ in Romans 8. Christ's death in Romans 6 can be experienced only by His Spirit in Romans 8. In other words, if we are not in the Spirit, reckoning that we are dead does not work.

Christ is Christ, and you are you; and His death is not yours unless you are joined to Him organically by the Spirit. In the compound Spirit there are the elements of Christ's death and its effectiveness, typified by myrrh and cinnamon. When we are in the Spirit, the compound Spirit, we do not need to reckon ourselves dead, because in the Spirit there is the element of Christ's death.

Some drugs have elements that kill germs. If you try to kill germs by yourself, you will fail. But if you take a prescribed drug, an element in that drug will kill the germs for you. The compound Spirit today is an all-inclusive dose. A medical doctor will tell you that the best dose is the one that kills the germs and nourishes the patient. This may be used as an illustration of the compound Spirit. In the compound Spirit there are the death of Christ, which is the killing power, and the resurrection of Christ, which is the nourishing source of the divine life. These killing, nourishing elements are compounded together in this one Spirit.

The Spirit of Jesus

The Holy Spirit is called the Spirit of Jesus in Acts 16:6-7. Jesus was a man who suffered persecution. As an evangelist, Paul went out to preach, and he also suffered. In that suffering he needed the Spirit of Jesus because in the Spirit of Jesus there is the suffering element. If you go to a heathen country to preach the gospel, you need the Spirit of Jesus to face the opposition and persecution. The suffering strength to withstand persecution is in the Spirit of Jesus.

The Spirit of Christ

In Acts 16 for persecution Paul needed the Spirit of Jesus, but in Romans 8 in resurrection there is the Spirit of Christ. In Romans 8:9-10 we have three titles: *the Spirit of God, the Spirit of Christ,* and *Christ.* These three titles are interchangeably used. This indicates that the Spirit of God is the Spirit of Christ, and the Spirit of Christ is just Christ Himself. These three titles are synonyms. The Holy Spirit of God is not only the Spirit of God but also the Spirit of the suffering Jesus and the Spirit of the resurrected Christ. As long as we have such a Spirit, we have the suffering power to face persecution and the resurrection power to live a resurrected life over sin and death (v. 2).

The Spirit of Jesus Christ

In Philippians 1:19 Paul refers to the "bountiful supply of the Spirit of Jesus Christ." The bountiful supply is with the Spirit of Jesus Christ. This Spirit brought Jesus through incarnation and through human living on earth for thirty-three and a half years. The Lord Jesus lived a holy, sinless life for many years by the Spirit within. This same Spirit brought Jesus through death and into resurrection. Then the Spirit of God became the Spirit of Jesus Christ. Through such a long process, the elements of humanity, of human living and suffering, of Christ's crucifixion, of His resurrection, and even of His ascension have all been compounded with this one Spirit.

The Spirit we have received is not merely the Spirit of God, possessing solely the divine element. The Spirit we Christians have received is the Spirit compounded with divinity, humanity, human living, suffering, crucifixion, resurrection, and ascension. God is in the Spirit. The uplifted humanity of Jesus and His human living and suffering are also in the Spirit. Christ's death, resurrection, and ascension are all in this one Spirit, so with this Spirit there is the bountiful supply. Paul could suffer persecution and imprisonment because of the bountiful supply of the Spirit of Jesus Christ. This supply became his personal and daily salvation. Even in chains and prison he still magnified Christ and lived Christ (vv. 19-21a). He magnified Christ not by his energy or by his own strength but by the bountiful supply of the Spirit of Jesus Christ.

The Spirit of the Lord

The Spirit of the Lord (2 Cor. 3:17) indicates that the ascension of Christ is compounded with the Spirit. *The Lord* in this verse refers to the crucified, resurrected, and ascended Christ. In His exaltation He was made Lord (Acts 2:36).

Second Corinthians 3:17 says, "The Lord is the Spirit, and where the Spirit of the Lord is, there is freedom." First, it shows us that the two are one, and second, it shows us that the two are still two. Likewise, John 1:1 says, "In the beginning was the Word, and the Word was with God, and the Word was God." The Word and God are one, yet the Word was with God, which indicates that They are two.

The Spirit Identical to the Lord

The Spirit is identical to the Lord. In the past the term *the pneumatic Christ* was used in Christology. *The pneumatic Christ* indicates that Christ Himself is the Spirit. However, do not think that when the Bible says that the Lord is the Spirit, it annuls the distinction between the Son and the Spirit. They are one yet still two. They are one yet still distinct.

Every truth in the Bible has two sides. Regarding the Triune God, if you stand too far on the side of one, you are

modalistic. If you stand too far on the side of three, you are tritheistic. We stand on the Word, so we are neither tritheistic
nor modalistic. We believe in the genuine Trinity, that God is
three-one. God is uniquely one, yet His Godhead is of the Trinity. The word *triune* comes from Latin. *Tri-* means "three";
-une means "one." Hence, *triune* means "three-one."

In John 14:23 the Lord Jesus said that whoever loves Him,
He and the Father will come to this one and make an abode
with him. Also, in John 14:17 the Lord Jesus said that the
Spirit as the Spirit of reality will come to abide in the believers.
Thus, in the same chapter we are told that the Father and the
Son will make an abode with him who loves Him and that the
Spirit abides in the one who loves Him. This shows us that
the three are in the believers simultaneously. The Triune God
is in us. This is a mystery, but by our experience we know that
this is so.

In Matthew 28:19 the Lord Jesus said, "Go therefore and
disciple all the nations, baptizing them into the name [singu-
lar] of the Father and of the Son and of the Holy Spirit." The
same Greek preposition for *into* is also used in Romans 6:3.
When we were baptized into Christ, we were baptized into His
death. Matthew 28:19 charges us to baptize new believers into
the name of the Triune God. M. R. Vincent says, "Baptizing
into the name of the Holy Trinity implies a spiritual and mys-
tical union with him." He further says that the name "is equiv-
alent to his person." To be baptized into the divine name is to
be immersed in the divine person.

A note in the Scofield Reference Bible says, "Father, Son,
and Holy Spirit is the final name of the one true God." Some
translations do not have *of* three times, just "the name of the
Father and the Son and the Holy Spirit." Our God is triune—
the Father, the Son, and the Spirit. However, such a title, such
a name, was not revealed until after Jesus' resurrection. Matthew 28:19 was spoken after the resurrection of the glorified
Jesus. It was revealed after the process of our Savior from
incarnation through resurrection was completed.

Before the resurrection of Christ, such a Spirit, the compound Spirit, was not yet (John 7:39). But after His resurrection the Spirit of God was compounded, and He is now the

compound, all-inclusive, processed Spirit. This compound Spirit, who is identical to the Lord, is, as revealed in 2 Corinthians 3, the life-giving, liberating, and transforming Spirit, who gives us the divine life (v. 6), liberates us from the bondage of law (v. 17), and transforms us into the image of Christ from glory to glory (v. 18).

The Life-giving Spirit

Paul says that the last Adam, through His resurrection and in His resurrection, became a life-giving Spirit (1 Cor. 15:45). He became not only a Spirit but specifically a life-giving Spirit. *Life-giving* shows what kind of Spirit He is. In 2 Corinthians 3:6 Paul says that the Spirit gives life. John 6:63 says, "It is the Spirit who gives life." Darby's New Translation has a parenthesis from verse 7 through verse 16 of 2 Corinthians 3. If we consider this section as parenthetical, verse 17 continues verse 6. The Spirit gives life (v. 6), and the Lord is the Spirit (v. 17).

Many writers agree that in Paul's Epistles the resurrected Christ is identical to the Spirit. However, this does not annul the distinction between Christ and the Spirit. There is always a twofoldness to truth. In 2 Corinthians 3:17 the Lord and the Spirit are one. In 2 Corinthians 13:14 we have the grace of the Lord Jesus Christ, the love of God, and the fellowship of the Holy Spirit. Here it can be seen that Christ and the Spirit are distinct.

The Spirit of Life

First Corinthians 15:45 refers to Christ as the life-giving Spirit. Surely there cannot be two Spirits who give life. Christ, the life-giving Spirit, is also the Spirit of life. This term is revealed in Romans 8:2. Romans 8 speaks of the Spirit of life (v. 2), the Spirit of God (v. 9), and the Spirit of Christ (v. 9), who is Christ Himself (v. 10). In this same chapter the Spirit is also spoken of as the firstfruits (v. 23).

The Seven Spirits of God

In the last book of the Bible the seven Spirits of God are revealed (Rev. 1:4; 4:5; 5:6). The Nicene Creed does not mention

the seven Spirits. In A.D. 325, when the Nicene Creed was
made, the book of Revelation was not recognized as part of
the Bible. The final recognition of the books to be included
in the Bible took place in A.D. 397 at the Council of Carthage.

Also, in Revelation 1 the sequence of the Trinity is changed.
Matthew 28 shows us the Father, the Son, and the Holy Spirit.
In Revelation 1:4-5, however, the Father as the eternal One is
first, the seven Spirits are second, and the Son is third.

Furthermore, Revelation 5:6 says that the seven Spirits
are the seven eyes of the Lamb. This means that the third of
the Trinity is the eyes of the second.

All these points indicate that in the last book of the divine
revelation the Spirit of God, for the building up of the churches
in a dark age, becomes the sevenfold intensified Spirit, who
carries out God's universal administration for the fulfilling
of God's eternal purpose and fully expresses Christ as God's
universal Administrator to bring in God's kingdom in the millennium (20:4, 6) and to bring the kingdom to its ultimate
consummation as the New Jerusalem in the new heaven and
the new earth (21:1-2).

The Spirit

This wonderful Spirit eventually becomes so simple in title:
the Spirit (2:7, 11, 17, 29; 3:6, 13, 22; 14:13; 22:17). In Revelation
we have the seven Spirits and the Spirit. In the seven epistles
to the churches in Revelation, the beginning of each epistle
refers to the Lord Jesus as the One writing to the church in
a certain place. Then the end of each epistle tells us to "hear
what the Spirit says." Revelation 22:17 says, "The Spirit and
the bride say..."

The Spirit is compounded, processed, and all-inclusive. He
is the consummation of the Triune God reaching His chosen
people. According to John 4:24, our God is Spirit. Not only the
Spirit of the Trinity is Spirit, but the entire God—the Father,
the Son, and the Spirit—is Spirit. God is Spirit, and this God
includes the Father, Son, and Spirit.

John tells us that when the Son came, He came in the
name of the Father (5:43). Then the Father sent the Spirit in
the name of the Son (14:26). The Son came in the name of the

Father; this means that He came as the Father. Then the Spirit came in the Son's name; this means that the Spirit came as the Son. The Son sent the Spirit to us from with the Father, and the Spirit proceeded to us from with the Father (see footnote 26[1] in John 15, Recovery Version). When the Spirit came, the Son was there, and the Father was also there. The Son was in the Father, and the Father was in the Son (14:10). When the Son was there, the Father was there. All three were there because They are one God. You cannot separate Them, yet They are distinct as the Father, the Son, and the Spirit.

THE FUNCTION OF THE SPIRIT

The Spirit is the reality of Christ (v. 17; 15:26; 1 John 5:6). When we call on the name of the Lord Jesus, we receive the Spirit as the reality of Christ (John 14:17), and this Christ, the Son of God, is the very embodiment of the Father (Col. 2:9). The Father is embodied in the Son, and the Son is fully realized as the Spirit. Colossians 2:9 says that the fullness of the Godhead dwells in Christ bodily. Christ, then, is the embodiment of God, fully realized as the Spirit. This is revealed in John 16:13-15.

The Spirit gives life to the believers (1 Cor. 15:45; 2 Cor. 3:6) and regenerates them in their spirit (John 3:5-6). He anoints the believers (2 Cor. 1:21), seals them (Eph. 1:13; 4:30; 2 Cor. 1:22a), and is Himself a pledge of God given to them (v. 22b). By this anointing, which brings in the divine element, He fills the believers. Sealing shapes the element into a certain form as an impression and becomes a mark. The pledge means that He is the guarantee that God is our inheritance. On the one hand, sealing proves that we are *God's* inheritance; on the other hand, God as *our* inheritance for our enjoyment is also guaranteed by the indwelling Spirit as the pledge.

He is also the bountiful supply to the believers (Phil. 1:19). He sanctifies us not just positionally but dispositionally (1 Pet. 1:2; Rom. 15:16) and experientially as well. He transforms the believers (2 Cor. 3:18).

All believers have been baptized in this one Spirit into one Body (1 Cor. 12:13). On the day of Pentecost and in the house of Cornelius, when Christ the Son, the ascended One, poured out the Spirit on the believers, that was His baptizing His Body into the Spirit. First Corinthians 12:13 says that we *were* all baptized in one Spirit into one Body. Christ finished this baptism just as He finished His crucifixion. All who believe have been crucified (Gal. 2:20). In the same principle, we were all baptized on the day of Pentecost and in the house of Cornelius. We have been baptized and have been given to drink this one Spirit (1 Cor. 12:13). Now we are drinking this Spirit. To be baptized is outward; to drink is inward. Outwardly, we have been baptized; inwardly, we are drinking of the one Spirit.

With the Lord's ascension to the heavens and the pouring out of the Spirit, the whole operation of the Triune God was completed. The Father planned with the Son and the Spirit, and the Son came with the Father and the Spirit to accomplish what the Father had planned. Finally, the Spirit came with the Father and the Son to apply what the Father had planned and what the Son had accomplished. This applying Spirit is the consummation of the Triune God. He is not just by Himself as a separate Spirit, having nothing to do with the Father and unrelated to the Son; He is the consummation of the Triune God, the consummation of the Divine Trinity, to reach us.

The Spirit's reaching us has two aspects: the inward aspect and the outward. The inward was accomplished on the day of resurrection. On that day the resurrected Lord came back to His disciples and breathed Himself into them (John 20:22). This was altogether for life, the inner life.

Fifty days later at Pentecost, He poured out the Spirit upon the disciples like a mighty wind (Acts 2:1-2). Breath is for life, but wind is for power. At Pentecost the disciples were clothed with power from on high (Luke 24:49). The clothing of the Spirit is like the putting on of a uniform. The uniform gives its wearer power, authority. A policeman with a uniform has authority to stop us. If he did not have a uniform, we would not listen to him. The Spirit as our life, the life-giving Spirit, even the Spirit of life, is also the Spirit outside us, poured upon us as the Spirit of power from on high. All of this has been accomplished.

THE CONSUMMATION OF THE TRIUNE GOD

This compound, processed, all-inclusive Spirit is the consummation of the Triune God. Whatever He planned, whatever He has accomplished, whatever He will apply to us is all wrapped up in this compound Spirit. Divinity is wrapped up in Him; Christ's humanity is also wrapped up in Him. His death, His redeeming, life-imparting death, is wrapped up in Him. His resurrection and His ascension are also wrapped up in this one compound Spirit who reaches us. Inwardly, He is our light and life; outwardly, He is our power.

THE SPIRIT AND THE WORD

God has given us two great gifts—the Spirit and the Word. The compound Spirit is the totality of the Triune God and all His doings. This is why I say that this compound Spirit, including His Word, is the ultimate consummation of the Triune God reaching us. The divine person and the divine Word are wrapped up in this one compound Spirit. All the blessings, all the bequests, of the New Testament have been bequeathed to God's children. These bequests are also wrapped up in this one compound Spirit.

Two verses in the New Testament indicate that the Spirit and the Word are one. In John 6:63 the Lord said, "The words which I have spoken to you are spirit." Also, Ephesians 6:17 refers to the sword of the Spirit, which Spirit is the word of God. Not only is the word of the Lord the Spirit; the Spirit is also the Word.

This is why in Romans 10 Paul says that when you hear the preaching of the gospel, the word is near you, in your mouth and in your heart (v. 8). For many years I could not understand what Paul meant. How could the word be in my mouth and in my heart? Eventually, the Lord showed me that whenever the New Testament is taught, preached, read, or studied by anyone with a sincere heart, the Spirit works with the Word. Through the Spirit the Word gets into your mouth. Through the Spirit the Word gets into your heart. Without the Spirit, the printed word could not get into your mouth and into your heart. When you exercise your spirit to pray over a verse of the Bible, that

verse gets into your mouth and your heart. You should not read
the Bible without praying. You have to read the Bible, the holy
Word, prayerfully. You should not merely exercise your mentality to study the Word. You must come to the Word with prayer.
You need not use your own words; pray the Word.

We all know that when we pray in this way, the word on the
page gets into our mouth and our heart. We receive enlightenment, nourishment, watering, strengthening, comfort, and life
supply. Also, the Spirit is applied to us as the consummation of
the Triune God.

The Spirit and the Word work together. We should always
touch the Bible by touching the Spirit. We should pray by reading and read by praying. Then we will enjoy the Triune God.
Our burden is not to argue or debate but to present the basic
truth to God's people today that they may know that our God
is actually the Triune God, not for us to understand but for us
to enjoy. We are presenting the truth to help the saints know
that our God is triune for us to partake of Him, enjoy Him, and
experience Him.

THE HUMAN SPIRIT

We also emphasize the human spirit (Zech. 12:1; Prov. 20:27;
Rom. 8:16; 2 Tim. 4:22). Just as we have a mouth and a stomach for our food, we have also a human spirit, which is our
spiritual mouth and spiritual stomach. In a radio the receiver
is crucial. We may have a beautiful, well-made radio, but if it
does not have a receiver, it is empty. We are a "radio" to receive
the divine riches into the "receiver" within us—our human
spirit.

We strongly emphasize these two spirits, the compound
Spirit of the Trinity and the human spirit within us, because
the compound Spirit is the consummation of the Triune God
reaching us for our enjoyment, and the human spirit is the
only means for us to receive such a rich compound Spirit that
we may enjoy the riches of the Triune God and experience Him
daily, even hourly. We are here for a testimony that all the
people of God today may have a clear vision concerning the
Divine Trinity and that we ourselves may partake of Him and
enjoy Him all day long.

CHAPTER FOUR

THE BELIEVERS

Scripture Reading: John 3:6; Matt. 28:19; Gal. 3:27; Rom. 6:3;
1 Cor. 12:13; Rom. 8:9, 11, 4; Gal. 5:16, 25; 1 Cor. 3:6-7; Eph.
4:16; 2:21-22; 1 Pet. 2:5; 2 Cor. 3:18; Rom. 12:2; 1 Thes. 5:23;
Phil. 3:21; Rom. 8:29-30; 10:8-9, 12

The subject of this chapter, the believers, is seemingly
simple, but actually it is mysterious. A medical student very
soon learns that the physical body is not simple. A person's
psychological being is even more mysterious. As living beings,
we have two hearts—a physical one and a psychological one.
We can locate our physical heart, but where is our psychological heart? Where are our mind, emotion, will, and conscience?
Where is our spirit? Where is our soul? We believers in Christ
are spiritual beings, and as such, we are a mystery.

DESCENDANTS OF FALLEN ADAM

We believers are all descendants of fallen Adam. We are all
fallen. We were dead in sin under God's condemnation (Eph.
2:1, 5; Rom. 3:19; 5:12; John 3:18). While we were dead in sin,
God afforded us a change. We heard the gospel and believed in
the Lord Jesus Christ to receive eternal life (v. 16).

SAVED

Acts 16:31 tells us that when we believe on the Lord Jesus
Christ, we are saved. A complete initial salvation has six
aspects: forgiveness of sins, the washing away of our stain,
separation unto God positionally, justification, reconciliation,
and regeneration.

Forgiven

After believing, the first thing we receive, the first bequest according to the divine testament, the divine will, is the forgiveness of our sins (10:43).

Washed

We have not only been forgiven but also washed. To be forgiven settles our case before God. To be washed takes away the spot, the stain, of our sins. For example, if a child got his shirt dirty and then repented, his mother would forgive him, but his shirt would still need to be washed. To forgive the child of his wrongdoing is one thing. To wash away the stain from his shirt is another. God, at our believing in the Lord Jesus, not only forgave us but also washed us. Hallelujah! We have been forgiven and washed by the blood of Christ.

Sanctified Positionally

As part of our initial salvation, we have been positionally sanctified, that is, separated by God from the world unto Himself. First Corinthians 6:11 indicates that we are sanctified first and then justified. Positional sanctification precedes justification; dispositional sanctification follows justification.

Justified

The death of Christ has fully fulfilled and satisfied God's righteous requirements so that we are justified by God through His death (Rom. 3:24). We are "justified from all the things" from which we "were not able to be justified by the law of Moses" (Acts 13:39).

Reconciled to God

We needed to be reconciled to God because, when we were sinners, we were God's enemies (Rom. 5:10). We have been reconciled to God through the death of His Son.

Regenerated

When we believed in the Lord Jesus and called upon His name, we were regenerated; that is, the very Spirit of Christ entered into our spirit and enlivened us (John 3:6; Eph. 2:5). Regeneration has made us children of God (John 1:12-13; Rom. 8:16), members of the household of God (Eph. 2:19). It has also made us members of Christ, members of the Body of Christ (5:30; 1 Cor. 12:27). We who have been regenerated are members of the Body of Christ and also the sons of God.

Regeneration took place in our spirit, not in our physical body or in our mind. This means that the Triune God is now in our spirit (Eph. 4:6; 2 Cor. 13:5; Rom. 8:9). What a treasure we have within (2 Cor. 4:7)! The Triune God has come into our spirit to stay (John 4:24; 2 Tim. 4:22; Rom. 8:16). Here in our spirit is where the unsearchable riches of Christ are.

To enjoy these riches we must call on the name of the Lord Jesus (10:12). If we want to be nourished, we can call "O Lord Jesus!" When we are at home and also when we are at work, we can call on the Lord's name. When we call, we touch the Spirit (1 Cor. 12:3). Many of us pray often, but we do not get the nourishment from our praying. This should not be so. We are not praying to an idol; we pray to the living God. He is the very God who is now in our spirit. When we speak to Him, He responds in our spirit. When we exercise our spirit, we realize Him within our spirit. If we merely exercise our mind and pray from our mouth, the Triune God within us has no way. He is not in our mind but in our spirit. We must exercise our spirit (1 Tim. 4:7). In this way we can experience this true, real, and living God who is right now in our spirit. The Triune God as the life-giving Spirit dwells in our regenerated spirit.

BAPTIZED

Into the Name of the Father,
the Son, and the Spirit

After His resurrection and before His ascension, the Lord Jesus charged His disciples to go and disciple the nations, "baptizing them into the name of the Father and of the Son and of the Holy Spirit" (Matt. 28:19); that is, they were to baptize people into the very person of the Triune God.

In Acts and in the Epistles, however, there is not one verse indicating that the apostles baptized people into the name of the Father, the Son, and the Spirit. Rather, those who repented and believed in the Lord were baptized into the name of the Lord Jesus (Acts 8:16; 19:5). To be baptized into the name of the Lord Jesus equals to be baptized into the name of the Father, the Son, and the Spirit, and to be baptized into the Lord's name is to be baptized into His person, the very Christ (Gal. 3:27; Rom. 6:3). To be baptized into Christ equals to be baptized into the Triune God because the very Christ into whom we have been baptized is the embodiment of the Triune God. The Triune God is embodied in Christ the Lord, the Son of God.

Furthermore, when we were baptized into Him, we were baptized into His death (v. 3). Baptism unites us with Him in His death and in His resurrection. Water baptism should not be the performance of a ritual. It should signify that we are putting those being baptized into the Triune God, into Christ, and into His death and resurrection.

In the Spirit into the Body of Christ

We have also been baptized into the Body, the church: "In one Spirit we were all baptized into one Body" (1 Cor. 12:13).

We have been baptized, then, into the Triune God, into Christ, into the death and resurrection of Christ, and also into the Body, the church. Actually, all these "intos" are one. When we are baptized into Christ, we are baptized into His death and resurrection, and we are also baptized into the Triune God and into Christ's Body. This means that we are now in Christ, in His death and resurrection, in the Triune God, and in Christ's Body. When we baptize people, we should point out to them that they are now in Christ, in His death and resurrection, in the Triune God, and in the Body.

We need the reality of the spiritual fact that when we baptize people, we put them into Christ. We can put them into Christ because Christ today is the very Spirit. When we baptize people, we put them into the Spirit, who is the reality of Christ. This is what baptism should be. Baptism gives us the position to say that we are people in Christ, in His death, in His resurrection, in an organic union with the Triune God, and also in the living Body of the living Christ. To have this realization of baptism makes a great difference in our lives.

INDWELT BY THE SPIRIT AND DRINKING THE SPIRIT

After believing and being baptized, we are indwelt by the Spirit (Rom. 8:9, 11; 1 Cor. 6:19). As He indwells us, we are drinking. The drinking fountain is right in our spirit (John 4:14, 24). We must turn to our spirit and drink by calling on the name of the Lord (1 Cor. 12:3, 13b).

We have the Spirit as the aggregate of the Triune God indwelling us. In 1936 when I saw that God was living in me, I was beside myself. I wanted to go outside, get up on the roof or run into the street, and shout to people, "Do not touch me; I have God in me!"

The Triune God is in us. He indwells us, and we are drinking of Him. He is our drinking fountain; this fountain is not in the heavens but in our spirit.

LIVING AND WALKING IN THE MINGLED SPIRIT

Now we must live and walk in the mingled spirit. Romans 8:4 and Galatians 5:16 and 25 refer to this mingled spirit. J. N. Darby points out the difficulty of putting a large or small *S* on *spirit* in Romans 8. Although he does not use the word *mingled,* he surely conveys the thought that these two spirits are considered as one.

In Galatians 5:16 the Greek word for *walk* means to have our being, to move, and to act. Here is the consummate charge of the New Testament: to live, to have our being, to walk, to move, and to act according to the mingled spirit. All that we do must be according to our spirit indwelt and mingled with the compound Spirit, not according to ethical teachings or moral regulations. To walk according to the spirit is much higher than to walk according to ethical teachings or moral regulations.

The moving of the Spirit is called the anointing. In 1 John 2:20 and 27 we see that we all have received an anointing from the Holy One. This anointing within us is true; it teaches us to abide in the Lord. The anointing that John talks about in 1 John 2 refers to the ointment in Exodus 30. The tabernacle and all its utensils were anointed with that compound ointment (vv. 26-29).

Today the compound ointment, the Spirit, is within our spirit anointing us, moving within us, all day. Even when we are arguing or when we are about to argue, the anointing within moves in us not to continue but to go to our bedroom and pray. One day a sister went shopping, but whenever she picked up an item to consider buying it, the anointing within told her to put it down. Everything she picked up she had to put back. Finally, she decided she had better go home. As she obeyed the inner anointing and went back to her car to drive home, she felt excited and happy. If we do not take heed to the inner anointing, we offend the Spirit. We must live and walk according to this Spirit who is mingled with our spirit.

GROWING IN THE DIVINE LIFE AND BEING BUILT UP

Few Christians pay attention to the growth in life (1 Cor. 3:6-7) and the building up (vv. 10-12) of the Body of Christ and of the church, the house of God. Spirituality comes out of the growth in life; the aim of the growth in life is the building up of the Body of Christ and of the house of God. Practically speaking, this means the building up of the local church. Without the proper church life in our locality, how can we be built up with others? We need to be where there is a church. Then within that church we can be built up with others to be God's spiritual house (Eph. 2:21-22; 1 Pet. 2:5). While we are being built up as the local church, we are also being built up as the Body of Christ (Eph. 4:16).

BEING TRANSFORMED IN THE SOUL

Our spirit has been regenerated, but what about our soul? We need to be transformed (2 Cor. 3:18) by the renewing of our mind (Rom. 12:2; Eph. 4:23). The mind is the leading part of our soul (Psa. 13:2; 139:14; Lam. 3:20). For the transformation of the soul, the mind must be renewed.

BEING SANCTIFIED EXPERIENTIALLY

The transformation of our soul is the sanctification of our disposition. The Lord sanctifies us in our spirit, soul, and body (1 Thes. 5:23). Our entire being is to be sanctified, transformed.

TO BE TRANSFIGURED IN OUR BODY

When the Lord returns, our body will be transfigured (Phil. 3:21), fully redeemed (Rom. 8:23). When we believed, our spirit was regenerated. During our Christian life on this earth, our soul is gradually being transformed and sanctified. Then at His coming back our body will be transfigured. Our entire being will then be fully conformed to Christ.

CONFORMED TO CHRIST

As the many brothers of Christ, we will be conformed to His image and be with Him in glory (vv. 29-30). We will no longer be natural in any part of our being. We are still somewhat natural in our soul and corrupted in our body; this is why, after the regeneration of our spirit, we need the transformation of our soul and the transfiguration of our body. Then we will be fully conformed to the firstborn Son of God as His many brothers.

GLORIFIED

Finally, we will be glorified in the divine life and divine nature (v. 30) to bear the glory of God for His expression in the New Jerusalem.

THE WAY TO ENJOY CHRIST

The book of Romans is a sketch of the proper Christian life. In chapter 6 are all the facts accomplished by Christ. He died, and we died in Him. He was resurrected, and so were we. In Christ these are facts. In Him we are joined to His death and resurrection (vv. 4-5).

In Romans 6, however, we do not have the experience of Christ's death and resurrection. We need to go on to Romans 8 to experience Christ in His doings by the Spirit. In Romans 8 are the experiences of the facts revealed in chapter 6.

Then in chapter 10 the word gets into our mouth and into our heart. First, we believe the word that reaches us; second, we call on His name (vv. 8-9). The Lord is rich to all who call on His name (v. 12). The word *call* in Greek means "to cry out, to call with a voice." In Acts the Christians were considered callers of Jesus' name; we know this because Saul of Tarsus had authority to arrest all those who called on this name (9:14). Calling on the name of the Lord Jesus designated the early Christians. They were not silent; they cried out the dear name of the Lord Jesus.

If we want to enjoy Christ and all His accomplishments, we need to call on Him. The way to enjoy Christ in all His doings is to walk according to the mingled spirit and to call on His dear name. Then we participate in Him, enjoy Him, and experience Him to the uttermost.

CHAPTER FIVE

THE CHURCH

Scripture Reading: Matt. 16:18; 18:17; 1 Tim. 3:15; Eph. 2:19;
1 Pet. 2:5; Eph. 1:22-23; 3:19b; 2:15; 4:24; Col. 3:10-11; Eph.
5:25, 29, 32; John 3:29; Rev. 19:7; 21:2, 9; 22:17; Eph. 6:11-12;
1 Cor. 12:12-13; Acts 8:1; 13:1; Rev. 1:11-13, 20; 1 Cor. 3:10-11;
Eph. 2:20

The church is God's ultimate goal. God's goal is not just to
have many individual believers. His goal is to have a corporate church that can be His house and the Body of His Son.
This church is God's expression. The church is both God's
household expressing God the Father and the Body of Christ
expressing Christ as the One who is the embodiment of the
Triune God (Col. 2:9). What we are going to cover in this chapter is an extract of the divine revelation concerning the church
in the New Testament.

THE *EKKLESIA*

The church is first an *ekklesia*. This Greek word denotes a
called-out congregation. In ancient times when the city called
its citizens together for a gathering, that congregation was an
ekklesia. The New Testament, beginning with the Lord Jesus
in Matthew 16, uses this word to denote the church (v. 18). The
church is a congregation called out by God unto Himself. The
Brethren prefer to use the word *assem*bly. I believe this is a
better word to use, because the word *church* in English has
been very much spoiled.

When I was growing up in China, we understood the word
church to mean a building with a bell tower. To many of us the
church was a building. Today many people think the same.
They say that they are going to church, meaning to a building.

This concept is absolutely off. We must drop this thought. The church is not a lifeless building but something organic, full of life.

The church is an assembly of living persons, not a physical building without life. However, to consider the church as merely a called-out congregation, an assembly, is still superficial. There may be a congregation, an assembly, yet without life. Today there are many large congregations in our society that are without the divine life.

THE HOUSE OF GOD

The church is also the house of God (1 Pet. 2:5). By this we do not mean merely that the church is the dwelling of God. This Greek word *oikos* means not only the house, the dwelling, but also the household. *Oikos* means both the house and also the folks, the family, that make up the household; thus, it may also be translated as "household" (Eph. 2:19).

God's dwelling place today on earth is the church, and God, as such a great Father, has a family, which is the church. For our family life we have a house, and inside the house we have the family. To us the house is one thing, and the family another; the house is the building, and the family is the people who live there. God's house and God's family, however, are the same. The house is the family, and the family is the house.

We as the church are God's house, God's dwelling place. At the same time, we are God's family. Both the house of God and the family of God are one entity, that is, a group of regenerated, called ones, indwelt by God Himself. These called ones, who have been regenerated by God with His life and who are being indwelt by this living God with all that He is, are both God's dwelling place and His family. This is more than an assembly. This is different from a group or organization of people. This is something organic—organic in the divine life, organic in the divine nature, and organic in the Triune God.

Some stressed the *ekklesia* very much, but they did not pay much attention to the organic aspect of the church. They did not say much about the church as God's family. We must realize, though, that the church is organic; it is the living house of God. Paul says that the church is the house of the living God

(1 Tim. 3:15) and that this house grows (Eph. 2:21). Does your house grow? Our houses do not grow. They depreciate. But God's house grows! For something to grow, it must be living. Anything without life cannot grow. Anything that grows is organic, with life. Hallelujah, we are growing!

In 1964 I went to Plainview, Texas, to visit a small group of saints. Then in 1965 I went to Waco, Texas, to visit another small group. Without faith I would have been fully disappointed. When the news went to New York, a dear brother with whom I had been co-working for a number of years said to another brother that he did not believe that these small groups in Texas would last. In 1968 I went to Lubbock, Texas. I did not see a big church; rather I saw something that needed much faith. By His mercy I did have that faith. Then the saints in Texas moved to Houston in 1969, and I went to visit them. The situation there was somewhat encouraging but not entirely so. My visits to Irving, however, in 1982 and 1983 made me excited. There has been much growth among the churches in Texas because the church is something living. It is the living house of the living God. It is not something of organization but something of life; thus, its growth is by life.

THE BODY OF CHRIST

God's house, the family of God, is organic, but in a sense it is not as organic as the Body. The church is the Body of Christ. A group of Christians may be an assembly but may not actually be the house of God, because they do not live in the spirit. They may say that they are the Body of Christ, but actually they may not be, because they are still living in the natural life. As long as we live in our natural life, we are not the Body of Christ.

When I was young, I heard of two or three elders who met together to talk about matters in their so-called church. Eventually, one threw his Bible, and another got up and walked out. Was that the Body? That was not the Body but the fallen flesh.

What is the Body? Look at yourself. Your body is the greatest part of your being. Nothing can be your body but you yourself. Dentures are not a part of your body; they are something extra without any life. Our real teeth are joined to our body not by organization but by life. They grow organically in our body. A member of your body is organic; it grows in an organic union with your body. Whatever is not in organic union with your body is foreign to it.

In like manner, the Body of Christ is an organism, not an organization. A podium, for example, consists of pieces of wood organized and fitted together. A man's body, on the other hand, is not organized but organic, full of life.

The church is not only the living family of God the Father but even more a living organism of Christ the Head. Christianity has fallen into a state where there is organization instead of life. There are millions of Christians on earth. They have been forgiven through Christ's redemption, washed by His precious blood, and regenerated by the Holy Spirit; they are children of God and members of Christ. Yet, actually, in their life and service what is seen is an organization, not an organism. Christ is organic, but "anity" is not. Any kind of anity, including Christianity and even "local churchanity," is an organization.

The church should be only organic, an organism full of the life of Christ. Whatever you do must be from the life within. You are living. You have Christ as the embodiment of the Triune God living in you. Do not move by yourself. Move by Him. Do not act by yourself. Act by Him. Sometimes when I have intended to visit a brother, I have been held back because I realized that Christ was not going to visit that brother. It was only I, the natural I, the good I, the I with good intentions; it was altogether myself, not Christ. Then I would pray, giving my position, my ground, and everything pertaining to this visit to the Lord. Then the Lord began to go with me. There are many who love the Lord and are devoted to Him and yet who do not realize that their natural life should be put aside.

In the new man, the church, there "cannot be Greek and Jew, circumcision and uncircumcision, barbarian, Scythian, slave, free man, but Christ is all and in all" (Col. 3:10-11). *All* denotes people. To say that Christ is all means that He is you, He is me, and He is everyone else in the church. To say that Christ is in all means that He is in everyone in the church. The new man, the church, is not Chinese, Japanese, French,

English, German, or American. The new man is Christ. Therefore, when we act as those who are Chinese, Japanese, Filipino,
American, British, German, French, or Italian, we are no longer
the church. In the new man there is no Jew and no Greek. Actually, in the new man there cannot be any Jew or Greek.
There cannot be any Chinese or any Japanese. In the new man
there cannot be any white or any black. If you still want to be
black or white, you are through with the Body of Christ. The
church is an organism. Therefore, we must act in our spirit,
totally repudiating our natural life.

THE FULLNESS (EXPRESSION) OF THE ONE WHO FILLS ALL IN ALL

Many Christians do not understand what the word *fullness*
means in Ephesians 1:23 and 3:19. They think that the word
fullness means riches. Ephesians 1:23 says that the church "is
His Body, the fullness of the One who fills all in all." Gram-
matically, *the fullness* is in apposition to *His Body;* this means
that the Body is the fullness, and the fullness is the Body.
Fullness does not mean the riches. In Ephesians the unsearchable riches of Christ are mentioned in 3:8. We must differenti-
ate between the riches and the fullness. The United States
has supermarkets full of the riches of America. The riches of
America are its products, but the fullness of America is a husky
American. This fullness is the expression.

The fullness comes out of the riches. However, if we do not
eat and digest the riches, we may have them without having
the fullness. The riches issue in the fullness through eating
and digesting. If we do not eat and digest the riches, we will
remain skinny and short. In like manner, the church is not
only the Body of Christ but also the fullness, the expression,
that issues from the enjoyment of the riches of Christ.

This fullness is the expression of the very One, the universal Christ, who fills all in all. Colossians 3:11 says that Christ
is all and in all. *All,* both times in this verse, refers to people.
In Ephesians 1:23, however, the "all in all" that Christ fills is
something universal. Christ is unlimited (v. 23; 3:18). The
dimensions of the universe are actually the dimensions of
Christ. How long is the length? How high is the height? How

deep is the depth? How broad is the breadth? No one can tell. The dimensions of Christ in Ephesians 3:18 are unsearchable and unlimited. These dimensions are the description of Christ.

Christ fills all in all, and we the church, by enjoying His riches, eventually become His fullness. If I had only a head, without a body, I would have no fullness. This fullness is my expression. We must realize that the church as the Body of Christ is Christ's fullness as His expression.

THE FULLNESS (EXPRESSION) OF GOD

In Ephesians 3:19 the King James Version says that we are "filled with all the fullness of God." The preposition *with* literally means "unto, resulting in." We are filled unto all the fullness of God. We are filled, resulting in an expression of God. *Fullness* here means expression. Paul says he prayed that the Father would strengthen us with power through His Spirit into the inner man that Christ may make His home in our hearts and that we may know Christ's dimensions—the breadth, length, height, and depth—that we may be filled unto, resulting in, the fullness of God, the expression of God (vv. 14-19).

The entire book of Ephesians deals with the church. It is the house or household of God (2:19), it is the Body of Christ (1:23), and it is the fullness as the expression of Christ and of God (v. 23; 3:19). According to chapter 3, the church can be such an expression, not only of Christ but also of God, when Christ makes His home in our hearts so that we may experience His unsearchable riches. While we are enjoying Him in such a way, we are being filled with all the riches of Christ, resulting in an expression of God.

The church today should be such an expression, issuing out of the rich enjoyment of the unsearchable riches of Christ. We are burdened for the situation among Christians. Where is there an expression of God? I hope that among us there will be such an expression. We all need to pray for ourselves as Paul did for us in Ephesians 3. We should bow our knees to the Father, that He may strengthen us into our inner man, that Christ may make His home in our hearts, fully settling down in every avenue, every part, of our inner being. Then we may enjoy His love, and we may touch and possess His dimensions. We will be filled with Him unto the fullness of God, the expression of God. This is not just an assembly or a called-out congregation of Christians. This is a group of people fully possessed by Christ and enjoying Christ to the uttermost, being saturated by Him and filled with Him to such an extent that they become an expression of God.

Whatever we eat we express. When I was young, I would sometimes visit my grandparents who lived at the seashore. They often ate fish, whereas our family hardly ever ate fish. Whenever I went to my grandparents' home, I smelled nothing but fish. One day I asked my mother why everyone there smelled like fish. My mother replied, "Do you not know that they eat fish every day? That is why they smell like fish!" We become and we express what we eat.

When we eat Jesus, we "smell of" Him (2 Cor. 2:15), we express Him, and we become Him. What is the church? The church is the expression of the very Christ whom we eat. All the fullness of the Godhead is embodied in this Christ, and this very Christ is our bread of life (John 6:48). He said, "He who eats Me, he also shall live because of Me" (v. 57). When we eat Christ, we live by Him. This Christ is the embodiment of the Triune God; when we eat Christ, we eat the Triune God. Our Savior, Jesus Christ, the embodiment of the Triune God, is our daily manna, our daily food. We eat Him, so we express Him. This expression is the fullness of the One who fills all in all. Eventually, this is the fullness of the Triune God. We can be such an expression by eating Jesus. Let Him saturate your entire being. Let Him settle in every room, every avenue, and every corner of your inner being—in your mind, your emotion, your will, your conscience, your soul, and your spirit, in your loving, your decisions, your intention, and your motive. Whatever you do must be filled with Christ.

To eat Jesus is simply to take Him in and let Him be assimilated into our being. To eat means to receive food into our being; to eat Jesus means to receive Him into our being. The issue of our eating Him is the fullness of the One who fills all in all and also of the very Triune God. This fullness is the church.

The church is not only an assembly, nor is it only the house of God, the family of God; it is also the Body, an organism of this living One, which eventually becomes His fullness and the fullness of the Triune God.

THE NEW MAN

Ephesians 2:15 says that Christ through the cross abolished "in His flesh the law of the commandments in ordinances, that He might create the two in Himself into one new man." Then in Ephesians 4:22-24 we are told to put off the old man and to put on the new man. This new man is the Body of Christ. To put on the new man means to live a life by the Body. Before our salvation we were living in the old man, in the old society, but now we are members of Christ, living in His Body. We should put off the old man with the old social life, and we should put on the new man, the church. In this new man there is nothing natural, nothing Jewish, nothing Greek, nothing of social rank; everyone is full of Christ, so Christ is everyone, and Christ is in everyone (Col. 3:10-11). There is nothing but Christ in the new man. Our life is Christ, our living is Christ, our intention is Christ, our ambition is Christ, our will is Christ, our love is Christ, and everything else about us is Christ. He saturates our entire being.

This new man, according to Ephesians 4:17-32, lives a life by grace and reality. These are the two main factors in the living of such a new man to fulfill God's purpose. God needs a new man on this earth to fulfill His purpose, to carry out His intention.

THE BRIDE OF CHRIST

In Ephesians 5 we have the church as the bride of Christ (vv. 25, 29, 32; see also John 3:29; Rev. 19:7; 21:2, 9; 22:17). Christ gave Himself on the cross not just for you and me individually but for the church. When we think about Christ's death, we usually consider only ourselves individually. Yes, Christ loved us and died on the cross for each one of us, but His death was mainly for the church.

Christ also nourishes and cherishes the church (Eph. 5:29). To nourish is to feed. To cherish is to embrace with loving care, full of warmth, like a mother holding her child in her bosom. Christ treats His church in this nourishing and cherishing way.

The great mystery spoken of in 5:32 refers to Christ and the church. Chapter 5 refers to love (vv. 2, 25) and light (vv. 8-9, 13). Love is the source of grace, and light is the source of truth. When light shines, there is truth. When love is expressed, there is grace. In chapter 4 as the new man, the church experiences grace and reality, but in chapter 5 the bride that satisfies Christ experiences something deeper and higher, that is, love and light. As the new man, the church fulfills God's purpose. As the bride, the church satisfies Christ's desire. He is the Husband, and the church is His wife, satisfying her Husband's desire.

THE WARRIOR

In chapter 4 the new man fulfills God's purpose. In chapter 5 the bride satisfies Christ's heart's desire. Now in chapter 6 the church fights against God's enemy as the warrior (vv. 10-17).

ITS UNIVERSAL ASPECT

The universal aspect of the church is mentioned in Matthew 16:18. When Peter recognized that the Lord Jesus was the Christ and the Son of God, the Lord told him that He would build His church on this rock. The church here is universal, comprising all the believers of all times and in all places, including Paul, Peter, and all the saints throughout these twenty centuries (1 Cor. 12:13).

ITS LOCAL ASPECT

The local aspect of the church was referred to by the Lord Jesus in Matthew 18:17. The Lord Jesus in the four Gospels mentioned the church only twice: once in Matthew 16:18, referring to its universal aspect, and the second time in Matthew 18:17, referring to its local aspect.

In Matthew 18 the Lord Jesus said that if we have any problem that we cannot solve, we should tell it to the church. This refers to the church in a certain locality. It would be hard to tell a problem to the universal church. Today many Christians who love the Lord care only for the universal church.

In their concept, as long as they are members of the Body of Christ, that is good enough; but we would ask, practically speaking, where is their church? If we have any problem that needs the church's help to be solved, where shall we go? We must have a local church that we are part of, from which we can get help and to which we may go with our problems.

The Local Churches

Universally, the church is one. But locally, the churches are many. In Acts 8:1 there is the church in Jerusalem. In Acts 13:1 there is the church in Antioch. Then there are churches mentioned in Acts 14:23 and 15:41; here the word *churches* is used because there were a number of cities in these regions. In Romans 16:1 there is the church in Cenchrea. There is the church in Corinth (1 Cor. 1:2). In Galatians 1:2 we have the churches of Galatia; there were several because Galatia was a province of the ancient Roman Empire with many cities. In Revelation 1:4 and 11 there are the seven churches in Asia. Asia was also a province.

Verse 11 says, "What you see write in a scroll and send it to the seven churches: to Ephesus and to Smyrna and to Pergamos and to Thyatira and to Sardis and to Philadelphia and to Laodicea." This verse reveals that a local church equals a local city. To write to the church in Ephesus means to write to the city of Ephesus. These are local churches. A local church is not a term used as a name, but it describes the fact of one church in a locality. The church does not have a name, just as the moon does not have a name. There is no such thing as an American moon or a Chinese moon. The moon in China is the same moon as in other countries. When it is over China, it is the moon in China. When it is over Britain, it is the moon in Britain. It is the one moon. In like manner, the church is one; it is unique. The church is both local and universal.

The Lampstands

These local churches are lampstands. A lampstand is the embodiment of the Triune God. How do we know this? First, the substance of the lampstand is gold, signifying God the Father and the divine nature. Then, the lampstand has a shape; it is

not just a lump of gold but has a definite form. This signifies
Christ as the very embodiment of God. Third, the seven lamps
are the seven eyes of the Lamb and the seven Spirits of God
(5:6; 4:5). The seven lamps as the seven Spirits of God are the
expression of the Triune God. The Spirit is the expression, the
Son is the shape, the form, and the Father is the substance of
the church as the wonderful lampstand.

To say that the church is the embodiment of the Triune
God is not to make the church a part of deity, an object of worship. We mean that the church is an entity born of God (John
1:12-13), possessing God's life (1 John 5:11-12) and enjoying
God's nature (2 Pet. 1:4). The church has the divine substance,
bears the likeness of Christ, and expresses the very God. Since
we have been born of God, we surely have God's life and possess His nature, and we enjoy this life and nature every day.
We are learning by His mercy and grace not to live by our natural life but by the divine life and nature. As we are thus being
transformed, there will be the fullness, the expression, the
form, the appearance, of Christ, and we will be shining, not by
ourselves but by the sevenfold intensified Spirit.

The church is the embodiment of the Triune God to express
Him. We as members of Christ are the sons of God born of Him,
having His life and possessing His nature. We are doing our
best to live by this life and nature so that we may be filled and
saturated with this rich Christ to become His expression
through the sevenfold intensified Spirit.

This is a local church. It is not just an outward assembly. It
is something inward, of life, yet expressing the very God. Dear
saints, this is God's goal.

Its Contents—
the Pneumatic Christ

The content of the church is the pneumatic Christ. Great
teachers in early church history used such a term. It means
that Christ is identical to the pneuma, to the Spirit. We cannot
explain this, yet it is a fact. Today you and I are living Christ.
Christ is not only our inner life but also our outward living.
Paul says, "To me, to live is Christ" (Phil. 1:21a). We live Christ.
He is not merely the objective Christ sitting on the throne;

this Christ who is on the throne at the right hand of God simultaneously is within us.

How can Christ be on the throne in the heavens and also be within us? Romans 8:34 tells us clearly that Christ is at the right hand of God, but verse 10 of the same chapter says, "Christ is in you." In the same chapter, one verse tells us that Christ is in the heavens, and another verse tells us that Christ is in us.

Electricity provides us with a good illustration of how this can be. The light in a room comes from electricity. This electricity is at the same time in the power plant and in the room. There is a current of electricity. This current connects the power plant to the building. Similarly, Christ is "electrical," pneumatic. There is a current from the throne of God to our spirit. Hallelujah! Our spirits are all connected to the heavenly throne, just as the lights in a room are all connected to the power plant by the inner current of electricity. The current of electricity is simply the electricity itself. The current is the electricity in motion. The moving electricity is the current. Christ is the moving pneuma. In his first Epistle, John calls this moving current the fellowship (1:3). The fellowship is the current of Christ. Christ is circulating, moving. We are short of the human utterance to describe something so mysterious and profound. Electricity, however, can help us illustrate such a mysterious, abstract matter.

Our Christ is the current of electricity. Our Christ is the blood circulation in His Body. He is the very fellowship between God and us and among all God's children. The current is the pneumatic Christ, and this pneumatic Christ is the very content of the church. Christ, who is the life-giving Spirit (1 Cor. 15:45), is always moving to impart Himself into us. The purpose of the electric current is to impart electricity into the bulbs so that they might all express the light of electricity. This pneumatic Christ is moving within us for the purpose of imparting Himself into us so that we may express His life. We all have been baptized in Him, and now we are drinking Him (12:13).

ITS FOUNDATION

The church's foundation is Christ, revealed and ministered

through the apostles and prophets. Ephesians 2:20 speaks of the foundation of the apostles and prophets. This foundation is the very Christ whom they ministered to others. Paul says that Christ is the unique foundation that he laid. No one can lay another foundation (1 Cor. 3:10-11). The Christ who is the foundation of the church is the unique Christ revealed and ministered by the early apostles, as recorded in the New Testament.

We must stay with this Christ. We should not take "another Christ." How grateful we are to the Lord that He has kept His holy Word on this earth and that under His sovereignty it has been translated into so many languages! What a mercy! If there were no Bible on this earth, what a dark age this would be. Hallelujah, we have the Bible! This is surely the lamp shining in a dark place (2 Pet. 1:19). It has become the light of our pathway (Psa. 119:105), and we are walking in this light—the light of the Bible.

ITS GROUND

First Corinthians 3:11 says there is no other foundation that can be laid except the unique foundation, Jesus Christ. Before a foundation can be laid, however, a house must have a site on which it can be built. The lot is the ground on which the foundation is built. Then the house is built on top of the foundation. The structure is built upon the foundation, and the foundation is laid on the ground.

The Catholic Church claims that its foundation is Christ. The Presbyterian and Methodist Churches also claim that their foundation is Christ. All the denominations make this same claim. Their foundation, however, is built upon different grounds. The Presbyterian Church is built upon Christ on the Presbyterian ground. The Baptist Church is built upon Christ on the ground of immersion in their water. The Methodists have a Methodist ground upon which Christ as their foundation is built. The various denominations follow the same way. They build their denomination on Christ, but on their particular ground.

We do not like to criticize, but we must speak the truth. I feel sorrowful that the Southern Baptist Church only recognizes those who are immersed in their water and by their pastors. If someone has been immersed elsewhere, they will not let him join them unless he accepts their immersion done by their pastor. This makes Baptist immersion the ground and makes them a sect, a denomination. The Church of Christ has a similar practice, except that they believe in baptismal regeneration, that their water can regenerate those who are baptized in it.

Before I came to Dallas in 1966, I was invited by a brother in Los Angeles to his home for dinner. While we were eating, a brother asked if I believed in water baptism. I said, "I believe in water baptism and in Spirit baptism as well." He immediately began to argue that there is no such thing as water baptism in the Bible. I had been a Christian for forty years and had never heard any Christian say that in the New Testament there is no water baptism. When I referred him to John 3:5 about being born of water and the Spirit, he said that the water there is the water in the mother's womb! To him everyone must first be born of his mother, signified by the water, and then he must be born of the Spirit. I had never heard such an explanation. The concept was so off that I felt there was no need to talk further.

The next morning I flew to Dallas. In the evening I held a meeting there. While I was speaking, a bold woman asked me about water baptism. I found out that she was from the Church of Christ and was totally for water baptism in their water. In Los Angeles someone had been completely against water baptism, and the very next day in Dallas there was someone completely for water baptism. Such is today's situation. People build a so-called church on their kind of ground.

All the different denominations came into existence on their different grounds. Their different names—Presbyterians, Baptists, Episcopalians, Lutherans, Methodists, Pentecostals, and others—are the grounds on which they build their church. On what ground are you being built? Do not say on Christ. Every Christian says that. Whatever denomination or group you go to, they will say that their foundation is Christ. But what about the ground where the foundation is laid?

What is our ground? The ground from the very beginning of the Christian era, from the time of the apostles, is the unique oneness of the Body of Christ, kept and expressed in each local church at its locality (Rev. 1:11). This means that we Christians, in whatever locality we are, come together to be the church there. We have no other ground than that of the unique oneness of the Body of Christ. A local church is an expression of the universal church. The church universally is one, and this one Body of Christ is expressed in many localities. In every locality where there are a number of saints, these saints should come together as the church there, not to take the ground of baptism by immersion, tongue-speaking, the presbytery, a method, the episcopal system, or any ground except that of being one with all others meeting there as a local expression of the Body of Christ.

This unique oneness should be the ground on which we are being built. We should not be sectarian; we should not be exclusive. We must be all-inclusive, open and loving to all the dear saints. As long as they are Christians, they are our brothers. Our brothers have been scattered to many denominations. In spite of this, we still love them. We should not have an attitude or spirit of fighting, opposing, or debating. That is wrong. We should always hold a spirit and an attitude of loving all Christians. As long as they bear the name Christian and believe in the Lord Jesus, they are our brothers and sisters. In the local churches we do not have any wall. We have no fence. We consider all the dear Christians as our brothers.

PREACHING THE GOSPEL, PRESENTING THE TRUTH, AND MINISTERING LIFE AS THE TESTIMONY OF JESUS

We must learn the truth, grow in life, and go out to contact people. What we say will depend on our discernment. If the person is not saved, we will preach the gospel. If we find out that he is a Christian, we can present the truth we have learned. Christians greatly appreciate the truth. Maybe we could present the truth of transformation as in 2 Corinthians 3:18. Then, if possible, we can minister life to him by witnessing, telling him how we have received Christ and how we experience Him as life. A testimony will minister life to people. Do not expect to bring people to the meeting to have an increase for the church. Leave the matter of increase in the Lord's hands. Our testimony is not a great number. Our testimony is a group of saints living in the spirit, walking according to the spirit, and being the living expression of Jesus in the family, at school, on the job, and in the church life. Our burden is to present the gospel to the unsaved, the truth to the saved, and life to the seeking ones. Leave the church matter to the Lord. Let each person choose for himself according to his discernment. No one can manage today's Christianity. It is too big. We have to realize our smallness. We are to live Christ and walk in the spirit, being the living testimony to Him. In this way we will be a benefit to all those whom we contact. We should not expect to have them come to our meeting. If they would like to come, of course we do not refuse them. I hope that we are all clear about where we stand and how we practice the church life. May the Lord bless us all.

CHAPTER SIX

THE KINGDOM

(1)

Scripture Reading: Matt. 3:1-2; 4:17; 10:1, 7; Luke 10:1, 9, 11; 4:43; Matt. 24:14; Luke 17:20-21; John 3:3, 5; Mark 4:26-29; Acts 1:3; 8:12; 19:8; 20:25; 28:23, 30-31; Rom. 14:17; 1 Cor. 4:17, 20; 6:9-10; Gal. 5:21; Eph. 5:5; 2 Pet. 1:3, 11; Rev. 1:9

THE CHURCH AND THE KINGDOM

The Father's plan, the Son's redemption, and the Spirit's application produce the believers, who are the components of the church. In Matthew 16:18-19 the Lord Jesus told Peter, "Upon this rock I will build My church, and...I will give to you the keys of the kingdom of the heavens" to open the doors of the kingdom. Peter used one key on the day of Pentecost to open the gate for the Jewish believers to enter the kingdom of the heavens (Acts 2:38-42); he used the other in the house of Cornelius to open the gate for the Gentile believers to enter the kingdom (10:34-48). In Matthew 16:18-19 these two terms, *the church* and *the kingdom,* are interchangeable. Where there is the church, surely there is the kingdom. If there is the kingdom, surely there is the church.

A CHART OF THE KINGDOM

Since the kingdom is one of the most complicated subjects in the Bible, the chart on the following pages will be a great help to our understanding. The first and last circles of the chart are colored golden yellow. Gold signifies God or what is divine. These two circles represent eternity past and eternity future. In between these two circles are four circles in time.

A CHART SHOWING
BETWEEN THE KINGDOM OF THE

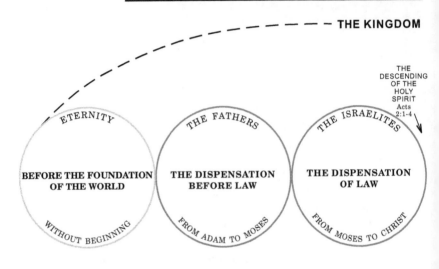

THE KINGDOM

THE DESCENDING OF THE HOLY SPIRIT
Acts 2:1-4

ETERNITY

THE FATHERS

THE ISRAELITES

BEFORE THE FOUNDATION OF THE WORLD

THE DISPENSATION BEFORE LAW

THE DISPENSATION OF LAW

WITHOUT BEGINNING

FROM ADAM TO MOSES

FROM MOSES TO CHRIST

ETERNITY PAST	FROM THE CREATION OF ADAM TO THE DECREE OF THE LAW	FROM THE DECREE OF THE LAW TO THE COMING OF GRACE
Eph. 1:4 1 Pet. 1:20	Rom. 5:13-14	John 1:17

THE DIFFERENCE
HEAVENS AND THE KINGDOM OF GOD

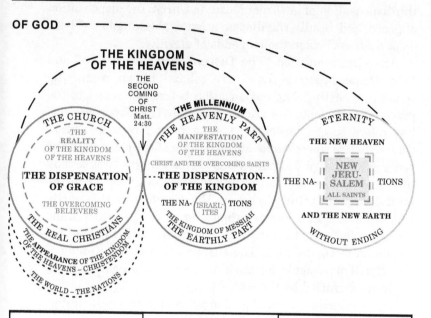

OF GOD

THE KINGDOM
OF THE HEAVENS

THE SECOND COMING OF CHRIST
Matt. 24:30

THE CHURCH

THE REALITY
OF THE KINGDOM
OF THE HEAVENS

THE DISPENSATION
OF GRACE

THE OVERCOMING
BELIEVERS

THE REAL CHRISTIANS
THE APPEARANCE OF THE KINGDOM
OF THE HEAVENS – CHRISTENDOM
THE WORLD – THE NATIONS

THE MILLENNIUM

THE HEAVENLY PART

THE MANIFESTATION
OF THE KINGDOM
OF THE HEAVENS

CHRIST AND THE OVERCOMING SAINTS

THE DISPENSATION
OF THE KINGDOM

THE NA- ISRAEL-ITES TIONS

THE KINGDOM OF MESSIAH
THE EARTHLY PART

ETERNITY

THE NEW HEAVEN

THE NA- NEW JERU-SALEM ALL SAINTS TIONS

AND THE NEW EARTH

WITHOUT ENDING

THE KINGDOM OF THE HEAVENS IS NEAR	THE MILLENNIUM Rev. 20:4-6	THE NEW HEAVEN AND THE NEW EARTH
Matt. 3:2; 4:17; 10:7	**(1) THE HEAVENLY PART** The manifestation of the kingdom of the heavens Matt. 24:46-47; 25:19-23; Luke 19:15-19; Rev. 2:26-27; 3:21; 2 Tim. 2:12	Isa. 65:17; 66:22 2 Pet. 3:13
THE BEGINNING OF THE KINGDOM OF THE HEAVENS	"The kingdom of the Father" Matt. 13:43 with Christ and the overcoming saints as the kings	with:
Matt. 16:18-19; 13:24; 22:2	**(2) THE EARTHLY PART** The kingdom of Messiah 2 Sam. 7:13	(1) the New Jerusalem as the administrative center Heb. 12:22 Rev. 21
THE CHURCH	"The tabernacle of David" Acts 15:16 The restored kingdom of Israel Acts 1:6	(a) constituted of all the redeemed and perfected saints, the sons of God Rev. 21:6-7
1 Tim. 3:15; Eph. 1:22b-23	"The kingdom of the Son of Man" Matt. 13:41; Rev. 11:15 with: (a) the saved Israelites Rom. 11:26-27; Zech. 12:10; Ezek. 36:25-28 as the priests Zech. 8:20-23; Isa. 2:2-3	(b) these perfected saints as the kings Rev. 22:5
THE REALITY OF THE KINGDOM OF THE HEAVENS	and	and
Matt. 5—7	(b) the restored nations Acts 3:21 as the people Matt. 25:32-34	(2) the purged nations as the people Rev. 21:3-4, 24, 26; 22:2b
THE APPEARANCE OF THE KINGDOM OF THE HEAVENS		
Matt. 13:24-42		

Time is a bridge between the two ends of eternity. The bridge
of time covers four dispensations: the dispensation before law,
the dispensation of law from Moses to Christ, the dispensation
of grace, and finally the dispensation of the kingdom. These
dispensations bridge the two ends of eternity.

The circles entitled "The Dispensation before Law" and
"The Dispensation of Law" are colored brown, signifying
something earthly. The dispensation before law refers to the
patriarchs and lasts from Adam to Moses. The dispensation of
law refers to the Israelites, lasting from Moses to Christ.
(Please notice the columns at the bottom of the chart with the
verse references and explanations.) From Christ's first coming
to His second coming is the dispensation of grace. Then the
Lord Jesus will return to set up His kingdom on this earth;
this will be the kingdom of a thousand years, the millennium,
the dispensation of the kingdom. The circles entitled "The Dispensation of Grace" and "The Dispensation of the Kingdom"
are colored blue, signifying the kingdom of the heavens. Heaven
is always signified by the color blue.

The last circle is colored golden yellow, but it is quite different from the golden yellow circle of eternity past. In eternity
future is the New Jerusalem, which is a composition of all the
saints from all the preceding dispensations. Some will be from
the patriarchs, some from the Israelites, some from the church,
and some also from the millennium. All the saints from these
four dispensations will be gathered together as the ultimate
consummation, the New Jerusalem. Around the New Jerusalem will be the purged nations as the peoples of the new
heaven and the new earth.

The Church—
Overcoming and Defeated Believers

The first blue circle of the chart is the church, which is
composed of the real Christians. Within this blue circle is a
broken circle also in blue. This circle signifies the overcoming
believers, who are among the churches and belong to the
churches. As Christians, our color is blue. We are heavenly. We
are on earth, yet we are heavenly. An American, for example,
may be in South Africa, but he is still an American. He is an

American in South Africa. Today we are here on earth, but we are not an earthly people. We are the heavenly people.

God has chosen and regenerated millions of people, but not all will go along with God. These become the defeated believers. Some who have been regenerated do cooperate with God. These become the overcoming believers. Among the believers, then, there are two categories, the overcoming and the defeated. Much of the dispute concerning the rapture is due to the missing of this point. The overcoming believers will participate in the enjoyment of the millennial kingdom, but the defeated ones will miss the mark.

In 1 Corinthians 5:1-5 the apostle Paul deals with a brother who is involved in fornication with his father's wife. This situation forced the apostle "to deliver such a one to Satan for the destruction of his flesh, that his spirit may be saved in the day of the Lord" (v. 5). His spirit, Paul says, will still be saved. Such a sinful person nonetheless was still a brother, chosen by God and regenerated. Paul commits such a one to Satan to be chastised, yet this person's spirit will still be saved. When the Lord Jesus comes back to set up the kingdom, could such a defeated believer be a king along with the apostle Paul? It is not logical to believe so. Nevertheless, his spirit will be saved. This case shows that there is a real difference between the overcoming believers and the defeated ones.

Four Categories of People

Outside the blue circle of the church are two dotted black circles. The first one indicates the appearance of the kingdom of the heavens. We call this appearance Christendom. There are genuine Christians and false ones. Among the real Christians are the overcoming ones and the defeated ones. The real and the nominal Christians make up what is termed *Christendom*. There is a difference between Christendom and the church as the Body of Christ. The Body of Christ as the genuine church comprises only the true believers. The nominal, false believers are not members of Christ's Body. They are in Christendom, but they are not in the church.

The second dotted black circle, underneath "The Appearance of the Kingdom of the Heavens," signifies the world, the nations. Among the nations is Christendom, composed of the real and false believers. The genuine Christians are the real members of the Body of Christ, which is the church. Among these genuine Christians there are the overcoming ones and the defeated ones. Among the nations is Christendom. Within Christendom is the church, a composition of the genuine Christians and not including the merely nominal ones. Among the real Christians are the overcomers. On this earth today there are these four categories of people—the worldly people, the nominal Christians, the real Christians, and the overcoming Christians.

Overcoming—
Going Along with God's Transforming Work

God's desire is to have a people who will go along with Him to overcome Satan and all the negative things. This is possible for us not in ourselves but by His full salvation. To overcome is to experience this full salvation. This salvation includes our spirit's regeneration and our soul's full transformation, issuing in our body's transfiguration. To say this is easy, but to experience this needs much work of grace.

We have been regenerated in our spirit, and we are being transformed in our soul. Whether we overcome or are defeated depends upon the transformation of the soul. If we let the Triune God as the life-giving Spirit transform us day after day, we will be overcomers. Even now we are overcomers, because we are going along with the Triune God's transforming work. As long as we are going along with His transforming work, we are overcomers. When we do not go along with His work in us, we are defeated. Whether we are overcomers or defeated ones depends on our attitude toward God's transforming work.

The Triune God today is within us, working to transform our soul. He is renewing our mind, our will, and our emotion. There is no problem with our spirit; it has been regenerated. The problem is in our soul. God is concentrating His transforming work on our soul. What is our attitude? To obey God is to go along with His work of transformation. We are all here under His transforming work. When this work on our soul is completed, we will be fully matured. Then the Lord Jesus will return to redeem, transfigure, our body, and we will be in glory (Phil. 3:21).

Our Daily Life

The matter of the kingdom is very much related to our daily life. God's transforming work is actually His exercising of His kingdom. Many Christians have been distracted by soulish pleasures. We may also be distracted from God's economy by different forms of amusement, entertainment, or sports.

God the Spirit is working within us, trying to transform our thinking. For example, as a lover of Jesus, you know that you should not go to a dancing party. You may want to go, but the transforming Spirit is struggling within you. Something within you says that this is not the right thing for a lover of Jesus to do. Actually, that struggling within you is the working of the Holy Spirit to transform your mind (Rom. 12:2) concerning the matter of dancing. He also desires to transform your emotion in this matter. Your emotion should not be toward dancing but toward the New Jerusalem.

Do you cooperate with this transforming work? Sometimes the saints are defeated, and they go dancing. At that time they are defeated ones. However, you can take grace to cooperate with the indwelling Spirit and say, "Amen, Lord. I will follow You. I go along with Your move within me. Hallelujah! I will go to the church meeting." This choice involves more than going to the meeting. It means that you are transformed in your mind concerning dancing. Your emotion is also transformed: rather than loving to dance, you love to go to the meeting. This transforming also involves your will because you determined not to go dancing. You said, "Satan, I will not go to such an evil thing. I will go to the church meeting." By taking such a stand, your mind and your emotion and your will are all touched. To be touched in this way is to be transformed.

This illustrates how the Lord as the all-inclusive Spirit indwelling us is doing His transforming work. If you go along with it, you are an overcomer. Otherwise, you are a defeated one.

The Reality, the Appearance,
and the Manifestation

Within the first blue circle of the chart is the reality of the kingdom of the heavens. The overcoming believers are living in this reality. Outside the blue circle is the appearance of the kingdom of the heavens.

Three parables in Matthew 13 speak of the appearance of the kingdom of the heavens. The first is the parable of the wheat and the tares (vv. 24-30, 36-43). Wheat refers to genuine believers, tares to the false ones. The false ones are not in the church but in Christendom, the appearance of the kingdom. The second parable is the parable of the mustard seed (vv. 31-32). A mustard seed is an herb to produce food, but in this parable it grows into a tree, a lodge for birds, that is, for evil persons and things. The church, with its nature changed, became deeply rooted and settled in the earth. Outwardly flourishing, the great tree speaks of the enterprises of Christendom, which are the outward appearance of the kingdom of the heavens. The third parable is the parable of the leaven (v. 33), which a woman took and hid in three measures of meal. Bread that is leavened is easier to eat. Many Bible truths concerning Christ have been leavened by Christendom. These leavened teachings are easier for people to take.

The second blue circle on the chart is the manifestation of the kingdom of the heavens. This is the third aspect of the kingdom of the heavens.

To see these three aspects—the reality, the appearance, and the manifestation—will help us to understand the truth concerning the kingdom of the heavens in a proper way.

THE GOVERNMENT OF GOD

The kingdom is the ruling, the government, of God (Acts 26:18; Col. 1:13). Here God can exercise His authority for the fulfillment of His purpose (Matt. 6:13b). The Lord Jesus prayed in Matthew 6:10, "Your kingdom come; Your will be done." If there is no kingdom, God has no way to accomplish His will. God needs a kingdom to accomplish His purpose.

MAN TO RULE FOR GOD

The purposes in God's creation of man can be seen in Genesis 1:26-28. First, God created man in His own image. This indicates that God's intention was to express Himself through the man He had created. Second, God intended man to have dominion (to rule) over all created things for His kingdom.

THE KINGDOM AND ISRAEL

The kingdom was first formed among the children of Israel. In Exodus 19:6 the Lord told the children of Israel that they would be unto Him a kingdom of priests. Israel was the kingdom of God in the Old Testament.

THE FIRST THING PREACHED IN THE NEW TESTAMENT

The kingdom was the first thing preached in the New Testament (Matt. 3:1-2; 4:17; Luke 9:1-2; 10:1, 9, 11; 9:60). John the Baptist, the first preacher of the New Testament age, told people, "Repent, for the kingdom of the heavens has drawn near." The first item preached in the New Testament is the kingdom, not heaven.

Many Christians think that heaven and the kingdom are synonymous. They believe that to be in the kingdom is to be in heaven. Many think that when a Christian dies, his soul goes to the kingdom of the heavens. To them this means that it goes to heaven. This thought is not according to the divine revelation. Heaven is not the kingdom; neither is the kingdom of the heavens heaven.

PREACHED AS THE GOSPEL

In the New Testament the kingdom is preached as the gospel (Luke 4:43; Acts 8:12; Matt. 24:14; cf. Luke 18:29 and Mark 10:29). The kingdom is the gospel. In Luke 4:43 and Acts 8:12 the Greek word for *preach* is the verb form of *gospel*. The word used in these two verses means to preach something as the gospel. The Lord Jesus in Luke 4 and Philip in Acts 8 preached the kingdom as the gospel.

In Mark 10:29 the Lord referred to leaving all and following Him for the sake of the gospel. In Luke 18:29, however, the

Lord spoke of leaving all and following Him for the sake of the kingdom of God. To leave all for the gospel means to leave all for the kingdom of God. Whatever we do for the kingdom of God is what we do for the gospel, because in God's eyes the kingdom and the gospel are synonymous.

INHERITING ETERNAL LIFE

From Mark 10:17 and 23 we can see that to inherit eternal life is to enter into the kingdom. To receive eternal life is one thing; to inherit it is another. The New Testament makes the difference quite distinct, but many Christians do not notice this difference. When we believed in the Lord Jesus, we were regenerated and received eternal life. When we live by this life that we have received, this life becomes our inheritance for our enjoyment. We receive eternal life today, but to inherit, to enter into, eternal life is a matter of the coming age. Whether or not you inherit eternal life as your blessing depends upon whether you are an overcomer or a defeated one. To enter into eternal life, to inherit eternal life, means to enter into the kingdom, to inherit the kingdom.

AN ENTRANCE INTO THE KINGDOM

All things which relate to the divine life have been granted to us for an entrance into the kingdom (2 Pet. 1:3, 11). Second Peter 1:3 says that "His divine power has granted to us all things which relate to life and godliness." Verses 5 through 11 show us the development of the eternal life issuing in a rich entrance into the eternal kingdom. By the eternal life with its development we may enter into the kingdom.

RELATED TO THE INNER LIFE
AND THE CHURCH LIFE

The kingdom is related to the inner life and to the church life. John 3:3 and 5 tell us that we must be reborn to see the kingdom and to enter into the kingdom. To enter into the kingdom of God is a matter of the inner life. We need to be born again in order to have the divine life. When we have this life, we are in the kingdom. To receive the divine life is to enter into the kingdom of God.

In Matthew 16:18-19 the Lord said that He will build His church and then that He would give to Peter the keys of the kingdom of the heavens. These verses show that the kingdom is for the church. Romans 14:17 says, "The kingdom of God is not eating and drinking, but righteousness and peace and joy in the Holy Spirit." Romans 14 is a chapter on how to receive the weaker ones in the church life. When Paul mentions the kingdom of God in this chapter, he is referring to the church life. The church life is the kingdom of God today. The church life, the kingdom of God, is not a matter of eating and drinking but of righteousness, peace, and joy in the Holy Spirit.

THE SEED SOWN IN THE GOSPELS

The all-inclusive Christ has been sown into His believers as the seed of the kingdom (Matt. 13:3; Mark 4:26). The Lord Himself is within the believers as the King, the seed. Jesus is the King; we are the "dom"! The kingdom is the expression, or the extension, of the King. The King is the seed, and the church is the extension, the "dom." The King's spreading within the believers as the seed is the kingdom (vv. 26-29). The kingdom was sown in the Gospels by the Lord Jesus in the midst of the Jews and within the Lord's disciples (Luke 17:20-21). The kingdom is something inward. We cannot observe it outwardly. The Lord Jesus said that the kingdom was not observable.

This kingdom was manifested to Peter, James, and John (Matt. 16:28—17:2). When the Lord sowed the seed of the kingdom in the midst of the Jews and within His believers, the Jews could not discern it. One day, however, three disciples went up to a mountain with the Lord Jesus. On the mountain Jesus was transfigured. His transfiguration was the manifestation of the kingdom. The kingdom is Jesus Christ Himself sown into us and growing in us until one day there will be the manifestation of the kingdom.

THE KINGDOM IN THE ACTS

In Acts the kingdom was taught by the Lord after His resurrection. Acts 1:3 tells us that He was with the disciples for forty days, "speaking the things concerning the kingdom of God."

The kingdom was also preached by the apostles. In Acts 8:12 Philip preached "the gospel of the kingdom of God." Paul also preached the kingdom of God (19:8; 20:25; 28:23, 31). The last two verses of Acts tell us that Paul "remained two whole years in his own rented dwelling and welcomed all those who came to him, proclaiming the kingdom of God."

Some Bible teachers believe that the kingdom has been suspended due to the rejection of the Jews. They believe that this is not the kingdom age but the church age and that the kingdom will come later on. This teaching is incorrect. As we have seen, the church actually is the kingdom. Even in this age, the church age, the age of grace, the kingdom is here. This is clear from the many references to the kingdom in the book of Acts.

THE KINGDOM IN THE EPISTLES

We can also see the kingdom in the Epistles. The Epistles tell us that the believers have been transferred into the kingdom (Col. 1:13; Heb. 12:28). Also in the Epistles the kingdom is the church life (Rom. 14:17).

First Corinthians 4:17 and 20 also show us that the kingdom is the church life. Verse 17 says, "I have sent Timothy to you...who will remind you of my ways which are in Christ, even as I teach everywhere in every church." Verses 18 through 20 say, "Now some have become puffed up as though I were not coming to you. But I will come to you shortly, if the Lord wills, and I will ascertain not the speech of those who are puffed up but the power. For the kingdom of God is not in speech but in power." These verses show that the kingdom of God is the church everywhere, and the church everywhere is the kingdom. The kingdom is here because the church is here.

Also in the Epistles some of the believers were the apostle's fellow workers for the kingdom of God (Col. 4:11). Paul and his fellow workers were working for the kingdom. This means that they were working for the church. To work for the church is to work for the kingdom, so the church is the kingdom. The church people will also inherit the kingdom (1 Cor. 6:9-10; 15:50; Gal. 5:21; Eph. 5:5; James 2:5; 1 Thes. 2:12; 2 Pet. 1:11).

THE KINGDOM IN REVELATION

The kingdom is also seen in the book of Revelation. John says that he was a fellow partaker with the believers in the "kingdom and endurance in Jesus" (1:9). If the kingdom is something for the future, then the endurance must also be for the future. If the endurance is here today, then the kingdom must also be present today. The mentioning of endurance in Revelation 1:9 indicates that the kingdom in which John was is not something yet to come. It is here right now; we are partakers with John in the present kingdom.

This present kingdom will come in its full manifestation after the great tribulation (12:10). Then, finally, the kingdom of the world will become the kingdom of our Lord and of His Christ in the millennium (11:15). This is a brief sketch of the teaching in the New Testament concerning the kingdom from the Gospels to the end of Revelation.

CHAPTER SEVEN

THE KINGDOM

(2)

Scripture Reading: Matt. 11:11; 16:18-19; 5:3, 10, 20; 7:21; 13:24-25; 25:1, 14; 19:28-29; 24:45-47; 25:19, 23; Rev. 11:15; 20:4, 6; 1 Cor. 15:24; Rev. 21:1-7; 22:2-5, 14, 17

THE DIFFERENCE BETWEEN THE KINGDOM OF GOD AND THE KINGDOM OF THE HEAVENS

The Kingdom of God

Most Christians do not realize that there is a difference between the kingdom of God and the kingdom of the heavens. However, the New Testament makes a clear distinction between these two.

The kingdom of God is the divine ruling from eternity to eternity. It includes Adam in Eden (Gen. 2:8), the patriarchs (from Adam to Jacob), the nation of Israel (Exo. 19:6), the church (Matt. 16:18-19), the restored nation of Israel (Acts 1:6; 15:16), the millennium (Rev. 20:4, 6), and the new heaven and new earth (21:1-2). Acts 1:6 and 15:16 reveal that the restored nation of Israel is called the tabernacle of David. The nation of Israel will be restored at the Lord's return. After this will be the millennium and finally the new heaven and new earth. The kingdom of God covers all the dispensations from eternity past to eternity future. In the chart in chapter 6 there are six circles, which include all the dispensations from eternity past to eternity future. The totality of these six circles is the kingdom of God.

The Kingdom of the Heavens

The kingdom of the heavens is the heavenly ruling from the

beginning of the church to the end of the millennium, the crucial part of the kingdom of God. In the chart in chapter 6 there are two circles outlined in blue, signifying the kingdom of the heavens. The kingdom of the heavens is a part of the kingdom of God just as Texas and Louisiana are part of the United States. Texas and Louisiana are the United States, but it is not correct to say that the United States is Texas and Louisiana. In like manner, we can say that the kingdom of the heavens is the kingdom of God, but we cannot say that the kingdom of God is the kingdom of the heavens. The kingdom of the heavens is the kingdom of God because it is part of the kingdom of God. The kingdom of God refers to God's reign in a general way, from eternity past to eternity future, but the kingdom of the heavens includes only two parts of the kingdom of God: the dispensation of grace and the millennium.

A Transitional Period

The ministry of John the Baptist begins the New Testament, but he himself was not in the kingdom of the heavens. Matthew 11:11 confirms this: "Among those born of women there has not arisen one greater than John the Baptist, yet he who is least in the kingdom of the heavens is greater than he." This verse indicates that John was not in the kingdom of the heavens.

Between the close of the Old Testament age and the beginning of the kingdom of the heavens was a transitional period. This was the time in which John lived. He was close to the kingdom of the heavens, but he was not in it.

Matthew 21:43 and Mark 12:9 indicate that the kingdom of God existed before the time of John the Baptist. The Lord Jesus told the Jewish leaders that the kingdom of God would be taken from them. At the time when the Lord Jesus was speaking, the kingdom of God was with the Jewish nation, but He was warning them that the kingdom of God would be taken away from them. These verses indicate that the kingdom of God was already in existence among the Israelites. The kingdom of the heavens, in contrast, had only drawn near (Matt. 3:2; 4:17). Here again it is evident that the kingdom of the heavens is different from the kingdom of God.

Beginning at Pentecost

In Matthew 13 there are several parables. The first one is
the parable of the sower. When the Lord Jesus came out as the
Sower to sow the seed, the kingdom of the heavens had not yet
come; it had only drawn near (3:2; 4:17; 10:7).

It is in the second parable, that of the wheat and the tares,
that the kingdom of the heavens is present. The Lord Jesus
said, "The kingdom of the heavens has become like a man
sowing good seed in his field" (13:24). The kingdom of God was
there during the preaching of John, of Jesus, and of His disciples. At that time, however, there was not the kingdom of the
heavens. In Matthew 3:2 John the Baptist said, "Repent, for
the kingdom of the heavens has drawn near." Jesus began His
ministry in the same way, telling people to repent, for the kingdom of the heavens had drawn near (4:17). In 10:7 the Lord
Jesus charged the twelve to preach that the kingdom of the
heavens had drawn near.

In Matthew 21:43, though, the Lord told the Jewish leaders
that "the kingdom of God shall be taken from you and shall be
given to a nation producing its fruit." From this we see that
the kingdom of God was with the nation of Israel from the time
of Exodus 19:6. At the time the Lord Jesus spoke the word in
Matthew 21:43, the kingdom of God was there, but the kingdom of the heavens had only drawn near.

In Matthew 16:18-19 the Lord Jesus told Peter that He
would build His church and that He would give Peter the keys
of the kingdom of the heavens. Peter used one of these keys
to open the gate for the Jewish believers to enter the kingdom
of the heavens on the day of Pentecost. Here is another indication that the kingdom of the heavens began on the day of
Pentecost.

On the chart in chapter 6 there is an arrow, entitled "The
Descending of the Holy Spirit (Acts 2:1-4)." The descent of the
Holy Spirit on the day of Pentecost marks the beginning of the
kingdom of the heavens and the beginning of the fulfillment of
the parable of the wheat and the tares. On the day of Pentecost, Satan began to sow tares, false believers, in the midst of
the wheat, the believers.

THE REALITY
OF THE KINGDOM OF THE HEAVENS

The reality of the kingdom of the heavens, as the reality of the church life (Rom. 14:17), is revealed in Matthew 5 through 7. John 3:5 reveals that regeneration is our entrance into the kingdom of God. To enter into the kingdom of God requires regeneration as a new beginning of our life (vv. 3, 5), but to "enter into the kingdom of the heavens" demands surpassing righteousness in our living after we have been regenerated (Matt. 5:20). Matthew 5 through 7 shows us the reality of the kingdom of the heavens.

THE APPEARANCE
OF THE KINGDOM OF THE HEAVENS

The appearance of the kingdom of the heavens is revealed in the parables of the tares, of the mustard seed, and of the leaven in Matthew 13:24-42. The appearance of the kingdom of the heavens is Christendom, which is filled with false things. The tares are the nominal, false believers. There are many such "believers" in Christendom.

Leaven in the Scriptures signifies evil things (1 Cor. 5:6, 8) and evil doctrines (Matt. 16:6, 11-12). Pagan practices, heretical doctrines, and evil matters have been mixed with the teachings concerning Christ to leaven the whole of Christendom.

Christmas is an example of this leaven. Originally, December 25 was the day that the ancient Romans celebrated the birth of the sun. With the spread of the Catholic Church, she assimilated this ancient festival because she had taken in thousands of unbelievers who still wanted to celebrate the birthday of their god. To accommodate them, the Catholic Church took December 25 to be the birthday of Christ. This is the source of the leaven of Christmas.

Christmas actually has nothing to do with Christ or the church. In the Lord's recovery we have only Christ. We do not have "endom." The "endom" is something added to Christ. In the word *Christmas,* the suffix *mas* is the "endom," the appearance of the kingdom of the heavens.

Easter is another example of leaven. As Christians, we thank the Lord for His resurrection, but Easter, a "Christian holiday" of pagan origin and filled with pagan practices, is leaven.

With the pope and the cardinals of the Roman Catholic Church we can also see Christendom, the appearance of the kingdom of the heavens. We do not want to be in the appearance; we want to be in the reality. If we live in the reality of the kingdom of the heavens today, we will enjoy its manifestation in the future.

THE MANIFESTATION
OF THE KINGDOM OF THE HEAVENS

The prophecy in Matthew 24:30 through 25:30 reveals the manifestation of the kingdom of the heavens. The millennium has both a heavenly aspect and an earthly aspect. The manifestation of the kingdom of the heavens is the heavenly part of the millennium. This manifestation is the kingdom of the Father. Matthew 13:43 says, "Then the righteous will shine forth like the sun in the kingdom of their Father." The righteous are the overcomers, who will be the light shining in the kingdom of their Father. In the heavenly part of the millennium, which is the manifestation of the kingdom of the heavens and the kingdom of the Father, the overcoming saints will reign with Christ as co-kings.

CHRIST'S DISPENSATIONAL REWARD

The kingdom of God is a part of God's eternal salvation to all believers, the entrance into which is by regeneration (John 3:5). God's eternal salvation includes His kingdom. To enter into this kingdom we need to be regenerated.

The kingdom of the heavens, however, is Christ's dispensational reward to His faithful followers, the entrance into which is by surpassing righteousness and the doing of God's will (Matt. 5:20; 7:21). The kingdom of the heavens is Christ's dispensational reward because it is just one period of time lasting one thousand years. We have received eternal salvation, but what about the dispensational reward? That is pending. It will be given to the faithful followers of Christ.

D. M. Panton once said that the Christian teachers of his day were giving out tickets for others to enter into the kingdom of the heavens. When they got there, however, said Panton, the gatekeeper would tell them that their tickets were not genuine. According to Panton, too many Christian preachers were cheating their listeners and giving them worthless tickets. Panton was very clear about the matter of the kingdom of the heavens.

Whereas salvation is eternal, the reward is dispensational. This dispensational reward is conditional. If a student does excellent work in his studies, for example, he will be rewarded at his graduation. He has disciplined himself to get top grades so that he may get a reward. As Christians, we must exercise ourselves under God's discipline all the years of our Christian life in order to receive the reward of the kingdom of the heavens. Many Christians today live in a loose way because they do not realize this matter of dispensational reward and punishment. Because of this, there is the need for the recovery of the truth concerning the kingdom.

In 1936 I published a booklet on the matter of entering into the kingdom of the heavens. Brother Watchman Nee encouraged me to write more on this subject. He told me of a backsliding brother, who, after reading my booklet, was revived and brought back to the Lord. As a result, in 1939 I put out a number of messages on this matter of the kingdom of the heavens.

As Christians, we must be careful not to lose our reward. Our salvation can never be lost. It is insured by God's predestination of us. Calvin was strong in the matter of eternal predestination, with which we agree, but he did not see the dispensational reward. Without this key there is no satisfactory way to interpret much of Matthew and the five warnings in the book of Hebrews (2:1-4; 3:7—4:13; 5:11—6:20; 10:19-39; 12:1-29). We need to pick up the key to interpreting these five warnings in Hebrews. The key is dispensational discipline.

Reward or Punishment

Christians will either receive a reward or suffer discipline. The reward is the kingship to be exercised by Christ with His faithful followers in the one thousand years. The punishment is revealed in Matthew 24:50-51: "The master of that slave will come on a day when he does not expect him and at an hour which he does not know, and will cut him asunder and appoint his portion with the hypocrites. In that place there will be the weeping and the gnashing of teeth." At the Lord's return the loose and unfaithful Christians will suffer punishment.

Do not think that the Lord is too kind to punish you. A good father always disciplines his children. Discipline is a sign of love (Heb. 12:6-7). We have been chosen, predestinated, called, and regenerated; now we are enjoying the Lord's rich grace. If we refuse to take the Lord's way, we must not think that when we die, all our problems will be over. This is not logical.

One day the Lord will return and set up His judgment seat. Here He will judge not the unbelievers but the believers. In 2 Corinthians 5:9 Paul says that he was determined to gain the honor of being well pleasing to the Lord. Then he goes on to say, "We must all be manifested before the judgment seat of Christ, that each one may receive the things done through the body according to what he has practiced, whether good or bad" (v. 10). At the Lord's return we Christians will have to render an account to Him at His judgment seat. His judgment will decide whether we will be rewarded with an entrance into the kingdom of the heavens or be punished in some way. The defeated Christians will suffer loss (1 Cor. 3:15).

The Need for Repentance and Confession

Christ's redemption is complete and perfect, yet we still need to confess our sins in order to be forgiven (1 John 1:9). As Christians, we need to repent daily to be brought back to God's economy. Many Christians have died with unsettled problems between them and the Lord. They committed sins after they were saved, yet they never confessed them or repented. God's forgiving and Christ's cleansing of the believers when they sin is based upon their confession. If we do not confess, God does not forgive. If we do not confess, Christ does not cleanse. To think that we may live carelessly and still have no problems after death is not logical. We will have to render an account to Him. The kingdom truth is very sobering. It wakes us up. When the Lord comes back, He will come not only as our Bridegroom but also as our Judge (2 Tim. 4:1, 8).

Overcomers

Among the believers in the seven churches in Revelation 2 and 3 are some faithful overcomers to whom the Lord promises a reward (2:7, 11, 17, 26-29; 3:5-6, 12-13, 21-22). These overcomers, who live in the reality of the kingdom of the heavens in the present church age, will be the faithful followers of Christ in the manifestation of the kingdom of the heavens. They will be rewarded with the enjoyment of eternal life in the millennium (Matt. 19:28-29; 24:45-47; 25:19-23). They will also be co-kings with Christ in the millennium (Rev. 20:4, 6; 2 Tim. 2:12).

THE MILLENNIUM

The millennium has an earthly part and a heavenly part. The earthly part is the kingdom of the Messiah (2 Sam. 7:13), the tabernacle of David (Acts 15:16), and the kingdom of the Son of Man (Matt. 13:41; Rev. 11:15). The kingdom of the Father is the heavenly part of the millennium. The kingdom of the Son of Man is the earthly part of the millennium. In the millennium the overcomers in the heavenly part reign with Christ over the earthly part. In the earthly part is the restored kingdom of David, where Christ as the Son of Man, David's royal descendant, will be the King over the children of Israel.

During this time the children of Israel will be priests (Zech. 8:20-23; Isa. 2:2-3). The overcoming saints will be kings in the heavenly part, and the restored nation of Israel will be priests in the earthly part, teaching the nations how to know God and how to serve Him. The nations will be the people in the earthly part of the millennium (Matt. 25:32-34). The sheep in Matthew 25 will be the nations, and the nations will be the people.

In the millennium, then, there will be three kinds of people: the overcoming saints as kings in the heavenly part, the restored Jews as the priests in the earthly part, and the sheep, the nations, as the people. The overcoming saints will have the nations to rule over, and the Jews will have the nations to teach. The nations will be the people ruled by us and taught by the Jews.

The kingdom of the heavens will end with the millennium

(Rev. 20:7). The kingdom of God, however, will continue for eternity.

THE KINGDOM OF GOD IN ITS FULLEST EXTENT

The fullest extent of the kingdom of God will begin in the new heaven and the new earth (1 Cor. 15:24; Rev. 21:1-2). In this eternal kingdom all the redeemed saints through all the ages will enjoy the eternal blessings of eternal life in the New Jerusalem as the sons of God and kings with Christ over the nations forever (vv. 6-7; 22:3b-5, 14, 17). As the royal family, we will have two titles: sons of God and kings over the nations. The remnant of the purged nations will be the people of the nations to enjoy the restored blessing of God's creation eternally (21:3-5; 22:2b, 3a).

Thus far, we have seen a clear picture of the kingdom of God and the kingdom of the heavens. Our God has a kingdom to carry out His purpose, accomplish His will, and exercise His justice. This kingdom displays His multifarious wisdom. Our God is just, wise, and purposeful. The truth of the kingdom will encourage us to go on, and it will also be a warning to us to be in the right place and on the right track so that we may arrive at the right destination.

CHAPTER EIGHT

THE NEW JERUSALEM—
THE ULTIMATE CONSUMMATION

(1)

Scripture Reading: Rev. 21:1-3, 9-14, 16-23; 22:1-2, 5, 14, 17

CREATION AND BUILDING

It takes the entire Bible to give us God's complete revelation. In Genesis we are told about God's creation. Then at the end of the Bible we see a holy city. At the beginning there is creation, and at the end a city. In creation God called "not being as being" (Rom. 4:17), but a city signifies something further because a city is a building. In God's economy, then, He first created. Following the creation, He began to build.

The thought of building runs throughout the entire New Testament. After Peter recognized that Jesus was the Son of God and the very Christ, the Lord told him, "Upon this rock I will build My church" (Matt. 16:18). Here is the thought of building in Matthew 16.

The thought of building actually came in much earlier. In God's consideration what was going on even in Old Testament times was a building. In Matthew 21 the Lord used the parable of a vineyard to signify the Jewish nation. At the end of that parable the Lord told the Jewish leaders that because of their fruitlessness, the lord of the vineyard would give the vineyard to another nation (that is, to the church) (vv. 33-43). The Lord said to them, "The stone which the builders rejected, this has become the head of the corner" (v. 42). The Lord was telling them that they were the builders and that He was the cornerstone, which they as the Jewish leaders were rejecting.

This rejected stone became in God's sovereignty the cornerstone of the building.

Christ as the cornerstone is the base of the gospel. Many preachers quote Acts 4:12, which says, "Neither is there another name...in which we must be saved." We must realize, though, that Acts 4:12 is based upon verse 11. Verse 11 tells us that Christ, the rejected stone, has become the cornerstone. This cornerstone is the very Savior in verse 12. Christ's being the Savior is based upon His being the cornerstone that was rejected by the builders in the Old Testament economy. The Jewish leaders until that time were the builders in the eyes of God; the rejected stone becoming the cornerstone is a prophecy in Psalm 118:22. In God's eyes, then, both the Old Testament time and the New Testament time have been His building period.

Right after His creation, He began to build. His creation was to produce the building materials for His building. God created the universe and man for the purpose of building a city. Creation means calling not being as being. A city, however, is a building of things created. God has two works. The first is the work of creation, and the second is the work of building. The New Jerusalem, a city as God's building, is the conclusion of God's entire revelation.

REGENERATED MAN, GOD'S BUILDING MATERIAL

For God to have a building, the center of His creation, man, needs to be regenerated. Regenerated man becomes God's building material. God did not impart Himself into any item of His creation. In His old creation He did breathe the breath of life into man (Gen. 2:7), but that breath was not something of His essence or nature. It was only His breath. That breath of life, *neshamah* (Heb.), became the spirit of man; as Proverbs 20:27 says, "The spirit *(neshamah)* of man is the lamp of Jehovah." Nothing of God's essence was imparted into man until the New Testament time and the completion of the full redemption of the Lord Jesus Christ. Then God came to impart not only something of Himself but also Himself into man that man might be regenerated by Him (John 3:5), born of Him (1:12-13).

When we were born of our earthly father, our father's essence and nature were imparted to us. We are now regenerated persons, the offspring of God. We are children born of God, not sons adopted by an adopting father. We have been begotten of a begetting Father. Whatever the Father is has been imparted into us, His children.

The only thing of His that we do not have is His Godhead. He is the very God. Even though we were born of Him, we do not participate in His Godhead. To say that we are deified in the sense of having His Godhead is blasphemy. We worship Him. We ourselves are not the object of any man's worship and never can be. That would be blasphemous.

However, we should have the boldness to say, "Hallelujah! I have God's life (Col. 3:4; 1 John 5:12) and God's nature (2 Pet. 1:4). In life and in nature I am the same as my God because I have been born of Him." His life is our life, and His nature is our nature. Hallelujah! We are the excellent children of God (Rom. 8:16; 1 John 3:1). The last stanza of *Hymns,* #608 says that with God we "differ not in life in any way!"

The natural material out of God's creation is not qualified to be used for His building material because it has nothing of God's essence. What God uses for His building must have His essence.

A GOLDEN MOUNTAIN

In our daily life we are bothered by dust. I like Texas, but one thing I do not like is that it is too windy. Too much wind brings dust. When we are in the New Jerusalem, though, there will be no dust. The New Jerusalem, the holy city, is a golden mountain (Rev. 21:18). This mountain is about thirteen hundred fifty miles high, the approximate distance from New York to Dallas. The New Jerusalem is twelve thousand stadia high (v. 16); one stadion equals about six hundred feet. Have you ever seen such a high mountain? It would take fifty days to climb it on foot, if you traveled twenty-seven miles a day.

GOLD, PRECIOUS STONES, AND PEARLS

The wall of the city is made of jasper upon a foundation of twelve different precious stones (vv. 18-20). Precious stones were first created and then transformed by pressure and heat. They are not merely natural but were created and then transformed. In the New Testament there is the strong thought of transformation (2 Cor. 3:18). The twelve gates are twelve pearls (Rev. 21:21). Pearls have also gone through a process. Pearls are produced by oysters in the waters of death. When the oyster is wounded by a particle of sand, it secretes its life-juice around the sand and makes it into a precious pearl. In this process we can see the death, the killing, and the secretion of the life-juice to produce a pearl.

The entire city is built of gold, precious stones, and pearls. There we will not need to sweep the floor. There will be no dust! All the created beings will have been transformed.

THE DIVINE BUILDING
WITH TRANSFORMED HUMANITY

In 1 Corinthians 3 Paul says that the unique foundation has been laid, but we must be careful how we build upon it. We can build with two categories of materials: gold, silver, and precious stones or wood, grass, and stubble (vv. 10-12). Wood, grass, and stubble all become dust after they are burned, but gold, silver, and precious stones do not.

In Paul's concept the natural created men are wood, grass, and stubble; and the regenerated, transformed men are gold, silver, and precious stones. When Peter came to the Lord Jesus, he was a "dusty" man, a man made of dust (Gen. 3:19), because he was born of the adamic race. Adam was made of dust, and Peter was born a dusty man. Nevertheless, the Lord Jesus called him Cephas (Gk. *Peter*), which means "a stone" (John 1:42). The changing of Simon's name by the Lord Jesus to Peter indicated that Peter would be transformed.

This was the reason that Peter was very strong in this concept, even in the writing of his first Epistle. He said that the Lord Jesus is a living stone (2:4), and that as we come to this living stone, we all become living stones to be built up as a spiritual house (v. 5). The spiritual house is not built of wood, grass, and stubble. It is built of transformed materials. Because our mentality is fully occupied by the natural thought of ethics, philosophy, and morality, we overlook this matter in the New

Testament. The entire New Testament, however, is saturated with this thought of the divine building of transformed humanity. The conclusion of the Bible is a holy city composed of gold, pearls, and precious stones.

THE TWO ENDS OF THE BIBLE
REFLECTING EACH OTHER

All the materials that comprise this holy city are found in the first two chapters of Genesis. In Genesis 2 there is the tree of life. By the tree there is a river. Where the river flows, there is gold, "and the gold of that land is good" (v. 12). There is bdellium, a pearl produced by the plant life, and onyx stone (vv. 9-12). Following this, at the end of the chapter there is a bride for Adam (vv. 21-23).

In Revelation 21 and 22 there is a bride, a city built of gold, pearls, and precious stones. Within the city is a river, and in the river is the tree of life. These six items—the bride, gold, pearls, precious stones, the tree of life, and the river—are all found in the first two chapters of Genesis. The difference is that in Genesis the city had not yet been built. The three materials were there but not built into a city. Some six thousand years later, through God's building work, all the materials have been built into a city. Do you see how these two ends of the Bible reflect each other?

In 1963 I went to Tyler, Texas, and stayed in a brother's home. After one of the meetings a friend of his, who was a traveling minister, picked up the phone in his home and called a brother in Plainview, Texas. He told him to come and hear me at any cost. The next evening he was in the meeting. That night I gave a message on how the two ends of the Bible reflect each other. This brother was caught. After the conference he said that he was clear to take this way. This was the beginning of the church life in Texas. I hope that we also can have such a glorious impression of the Bible's beginning and end reflecting each other. This is God's economy—to build up His eternal dwelling with the created things transformed to be His materials.

GOD'S BUILDING IN EXODUS

When the children of Israel had been brought to Mount

Sinai, God revealed to them the design of His tabernacle, and they built it. That was a type. In the Holy of Holies within the tabernacle there was nothing but gold to be seen. Gold overlaid the boards, and upon the ceiling could be seen the golden thread. Upon the high priest was the golden breastplate complete with twelve precious stones. The twelve stones on the breastplate had the names of the twelve tribes of Israel (Exo. 28:15-21). This was God's special "alphabet" to reveal His thought to His children by means of the Urim and the Thummim (v. 30). We can see, then, that the thought of God's building, using precious stones, is also in Exodus.

GOD'S BUILDING IN THE NEW TESTAMENT

In the New Testament we are charged to be careful how we build (1 Cor. 3:10-12). Do not use wood, grass, or stubble; that is, do not use your natural man. The church is not built of the natural man. It is built with the regenerated, transformed man. When you bring your natural life into the church, you make the church no longer the church. This is what is happening today. Many Christians, even Christian workers, are making the church no church by using the natural way, the fleshly way, man's way, not the regenerated and transformed way.

Peter tells us that as newborn babes we need to drink the milk of the word in order that we may be transformed into precious stones to be built up as a spiritual house (1 Pet. 2:2-5). John's writings especially stress this matter of transformation. In the first chapter of his Gospel there is the incarnate Christ as God's tabernacle (v. 14). Then in the last two chapters of John's Revelation there is the enlarged tabernacle, including not only Christ but also all His believers, because by this time they have been regenerated, fully transformed, and built together into one entity. Such is the New Jerusalem. This is the real revelation of God.

The Bible begins with God's creation and concludes with His building. This building is a regenerated and transformed entity. Pearls indicate regeneration. This is why all the gates for the entrance are pearls. Without regeneration no one can enter into the kingdom of God (John 3:5). Regeneration is the

entry into the kingdom of God, as is fully signified by the pearl
gates. The precious stones signify transformation. After entering this kingdom through the pearl gates, we are gradually
transformed for the building.

THE TABERNACLE OF GOD

The New Jerusalem will be the tabernacle of God with men
in eternity. The tabernacle in Revelation is not a new item. It
is fully revealed and portrayed in Exodus 25 through 40. Then
John 1:14 says that the Word became flesh and tabernacled
among us. When Jesus was on this earth, He was a tabernacle.
In the last two chapters of the Bible there is the eternal tabernacle. To understand the last two chapters of Revelation, then,
we must go back and study Exodus 25 through 40 and John 1:14.

THE AGGREGATE OF ALL THE LAMPSTANDS

The holy city, the golden mountain, is the aggregate of all
the lampstands. The entire city has one street (Rev. 21:21;
22:2), yet this one street reaches all twelve gates. How could
one street in a city serve twelve gates? Also, the wall is one
hundred forty-four cubits high (21:17), and the city itself is
twelve thousand stadia high (v. 16). These facts indicate that
the city proper must be a mountain. On top of the mountain is
a throne, from which the street spirals down to the bottom to
reach the twelve gates. It must be a spiral street, spiraling
down the mountain until it circles around all twelve gates.
One street, descending from the top to the bottom, reaches and
serves all twelve gates. On top of this golden mountain is the
throne as the center. On the throne is Christ as the Lamb with
God in Him (22:1). This Lamb is the lamp with God in Him as
the light (21:23; 22:5). This indicates that God is in the Lamb
just as the light is in the lamp.

This high golden mountain is a stand. Upon this stand is a
lamp; therefore, this is a golden lampstand. It is a golden lampstand with Christ as the lamp and God within Him as the light
shining out through eternity. Thus, the holy city, the golden
mountain, is the aggregate of all the lampstands, the totality
of all today's lampstands, shining forth God's glory in eternity
in the new heaven and the new earth.

The City and Its Street

The city and its street are pure gold, like transparent glass (21:18b, 21b). Transparent gold signifies the nature of God. Bible teachers generally agree that in typology gold signifies the divine nature, the divine essence.

Twelve Foundations and Twelve Gates

The twelve foundations of twelve different precious stones, bearing the names of the twelve apostles, signify all the New Testament saints, represented by these twelve apostles (vv. 14, 19-20). The New Jerusalem is a composition of all the redeemed saints, both Old and New Testament. The twelve apostles represent the New Testament saints, while the names of the twelve tribes on the twelve gates represent the Old Testament saints (Rev. 21:12-13, 21a).

Pearls signify the saints produced through the incarnated, crucified, and resurrected Christ. In His incarnation He was like a living oyster in the death waters. Then He was wounded by us, the little particles of sand. These wounds caused Him to secrete His life-juice around us, thus making us into pearls. Here is incarnation, crucifixion, and resurrection. Through this process we, the grains of sand, have been made into precious pearls.

Precious Stones

The foundation and the wall built with precious stones signify the saints transformed by the sanctifying Spirit (vv. 19-20, 18a, 11b). We were made of dust, but we have been regenerated into stone and transformed into precious stones. Dust, regenerated into stone and transformed into precious stone, is qualified to be used as God's building material.

The Length, Breadth, and Height of the City

The length, the breadth, and the height of the city are equal, just as the Holy of Holies in the Old Testament had three equal dimensions (1 Kings 6:20). The measurement there is twenty cubits long, twenty cubits wide, and twenty cubits high. This is the Holy of Holies in the type of the temple. The Holy of Holies in the tabernacle is ten cubits by ten cubits by ten cubits (Exo. 26:2-8). In both cases the three dimensions are equal. The principle is that such a building of three equal dimensions signifies the Holy of Holies, which is the very place where God dwells (Rev. 21:16). The entire city, then, is the very place of God's dwelling.

No Temple

John says that he saw "no temple in it, for the Lord God the Almighty and the Lamb are its temple" (v. 22). This indicates that the entire city is the temple. First, there is the tabernacle in Exodus. Then, after entering the good land, the children of Israel built a temple, which replaced the tabernacle. Even before the temple was built, in 1 Samuel 3:3 the tabernacle was called the temple. This means that the tabernacle and the temple actually refer to one thing. One could be taken down and moved from place to place in the wilderness; the other one had a settled location in the good land as a more permanent building.

The holy city is called the tabernacle. In the Old Testament the temple was in the city of Jerusalem, but in Revelation 21 and 22 the entire city is the tabernacle and the temple. This temple is not only God's dwelling but also the dwelling place of all His serving ones. At that time all the saints will be priests with an eternal priesthood. We will all serve Him (22:3). Our dwelling place, then, will also be the temple. The New Jerusalem is a great temple where both God and His redeemed dwell together.

The Glory of God as the Light
and the Lamb as the Lamp

"The glory of God illumined it, and its lamp is the Lamb" (21:23). "They have no need of the light of a lamp and of the light of the sun, for the Lord God will shine upon them" (22:5). The glory of God as the light and the Lamb as the lamp signify that God in Christ is the light of the New Jerusalem in eternity. In the new city there is no need of the sun, the natural light, or of any man-made lamp because God Himself will be the light, and Christ will be the lamp, shining out God to enlighten the entire city. This means that God in Christ is everything in the New Jerusalem.

The Throne of God and of the Lamb

The throne of God and of the Lamb is the administrative center of the city. Out of it proceeds the river of water of life in the middle of the street, with the tree of life as a vine growing along its two sides (vv. 1-2). The street is a spiral, and the river is in the street. Since the tree of life grows along both sides of the river, it must be a vine. A tree standing up could not grow on two sides. It must therefore be a vine, growing spirally along the street. John 15 speaks of the vine tree (v. 1). Jesus is the vine tree, which is the tree of life.

In a radio broadcast a Bible teacher was asked about the tree of life. He said that the tree of life is over. This is incorrect. The tree of life remains today, and it will remain forever. In Revelation 2:7 the Lord Jesus said that to the one who overcomes He "will give to eat of the tree of life." Even today this promise is being fulfilled. The tree of life that we are eating is Jesus (John 6:57). The Lord Jesus told us, on the one hand, that He is the bread of life (v. 48), typified by the manna. Then, on the other hand, He told us in John 15 that He is the vine and in 14:6 that He is the life. As the vine tree and as the life, He is the tree of life. The tree of life in Genesis 2:9 signifies Christ. He came to us as the reality in John 14 and 15. Still today He is the tree of life of which we may eat.

The tree of life as a vine growing along the two sides of the river signifies that God in the Lamb is the center of the New Jerusalem and supplies it with His divine life to nourish and satisfy it. The street, in which the river of water of life flows, goes down from the top of the mountain spirally to reach all twelve gates on the four sides of the city for its fellowship (Rev. 22:1-2). The street is for communication; communication is fellowship. First John 1:1 and 3 show us that out of this divine life comes the divine fellowship. The street, the river, and the tree of life are for fellowship. Today in the Lord's recovery we are in this fellowship, which is along the street with the river flowing and the tree growing.

THE BRIDE, THE WIFE OF THE LAMB

The ultimate consummation is the bride, the wife of the Lamb (Rev. 21:2, 9). The entire holy city is a bride. In John's Gospel, at a time when the disciples of John were jealous of Jesus, John said, "He who has the bride is the bridegroom" (3:26-29). As the friend of the Bridegroom, John was glad for his followers to leave him and go to Jesus, because He was the Bridegroom. Regeneration in John 3 is for the producing of the bride.

Consummately, we will be a corporate female for eternity (Rev. 21:2). The unique male for eternity is our God, our Redeemer, our Lord. We will be a corporate female to match Him. Eventually, then, what comes out through the twofold work of God—creation and building—is a couple. God is married to man, and man is married to God. At the conclusion of the sixty-six books of the Bible is Revelation 22:17, which says, "The Spirit and the bride say..." The conclusion of the Bible is that a couple says.

This bride who matches the Spirit is the ultimate consummation of all the redeemed, regenerated, transformed, and glorified tripartite men. The Spirit is the all-inclusive Spirit as the ultimate consummation of the Triune God. The Spirit is the Triune God reaching us, so this reaching One is the consummation. He has passed through the processes of incarnation, human living, crucifixion, resurrection, and ascension.

Today our God is a processed God. In the beginning was the Word, and the Word was God, and this Word became flesh. Incarnation is a process. This very incarnated One lived on earth in a poor carpenter's home. After thirty-three and a half years He was led like a lamb to the slaughter, and He was slaughtered on the cross. This was also a process. He went into Hades (Acts 2:27; Eph. 4:9), and He entered into resurrection. These also were processes. Surely all these steps are processes that He went through. Today our God cannot be the same as He was before the incarnation.

Do you believe that God is the same as He was before the incarnation? Hebrews 13:8 says, "Jesus Christ is the same yesterday and today, yes, even forever." If you say that since

His resurrection He is the same yesterday and today and forever, I agree with you; but if you say that this verse is true of Jesus before the incarnation, I do not agree. He did not have flesh before His incarnation. Through all these processes God became our Redeemer, our Savior, and our life. He has even become the rich, bountiful, life-giving Spirit within us today.

Thus, at the conclusion of the Bible is the consummation of the processed Triune God, and the wife is the aggregate and consummation of all the redeemed, regenerated, transformed, and glorified tripartite men. Hallelujah! The Triune God marries the tripartite man. Here is an eternal couple expressing the Triune God for eternity. The tripartite man in eternity will be enjoying this rich Triune God.

We were chosen and predestinated, and we have been called, saved, and regenerated. Now we are being transformed to be precious materials so that we may be built up to be a spiritual house to serve God and to be the Body of Christ to express Him. This is our goal. We are the children of God, being transformed that we may be built up as a house to serve God and as the Body to express Christ.

CHAPTER NINE

THE NEW JERUSALEM—
THE ULTIMATE CONSUMMATION

(2)

Scripture Reading: Rev. 1:1; 21:1-3, 10-21

THE KEY TO UNDERSTANDING JOHN'S WRITINGS

The book of Revelation is hard to understand. This is why God in His wisdom uses signs to make it known to us. Revelation 1:1 says that God gave the revelation of Jesus Christ to Him to show to His slaves; "and He made it known by signs." Signs are pictures. In teaching little children we make things known to them by pictures. Sometimes when I speak, I make things known by diagrams. John received a revelation concerning things so divine, so mysterious, so profound, that no human words could explain it adequately. Thus, the revelation was made known by signs.

Not only the book of Revelation but John's Gospel also is a book of signs. In our life-study of that Gospel I pointed out that the word *miracle* is not used. (Where the King James Version has *miracle,* the proper rendering is "sign.") The Lord's changing water into wine was a miracle, but John calls it a sign (2:11), indicating that it has a meaning. The Lord's changing water into wine signifies His changing death into life. Lazarus's resurrection was a miracle, but John calls it a sign (11:47).

John 1:14 speaks of the Word becoming flesh and tabernacling among us. *Tabernacled* is a verb. This sign gives us the key to understand how the Lord Jesus lived on this earth. He lived here as God's tabernacle. To fully understand the tabernacle, we must go back to Exodus, where several chapters describe the tabernacle. God's tabernacle among His people was not only where He dwelt but also where His serving ones entered to dwell with Him. This is Jesus! While Jesus was on this earth, He was tabernacling. God abode in Him, and all God's serving ones, Jesus' lovers, could enter into Him to stay with God. This one word as a sign describes what no plain word could express.

Also in John the Lord Jesus said, "I am the door" (10:7). Do you believe that the Lord is a door with a lintel and a post? A door is a sign, meaning that He is the very opening for people to enter in and for them to come out.

We must emphasize the very first verse of Revelation, which says that the divine revelation was given to Jesus Christ and that He made it known by signs. This is the key to open up the entire book. Without this key, the book of Revelation is closed to us. To understand the real meaning of this book, we must understand these signs.

THE MAIN SIGNS IN REVELATION

The Lampstands

The first sign in Revelation that the apostle John saw is the lampstands. In chapter 1 we are told that John, on the Lord's Day, on the island of Patmos, saw seven golden lampstands. The seven lampstands are the seven churches (v. 20). To describe what the church is in its spiritual significance would take a thousand books. But just one sign, one picture, is better than a thousand words.

What is the church? What should the church be? Look at the lampstand. The church must be golden. Gold signifies God's essence, God's nature. This means that the church must have God's essence as its substance. This gold must be in the shape of a lampstand, a lampstand shining with a sevenfold intensity. Some lamps have a three-way switch; but have you ever seen a seven-way lamp? The lampstand has a sevenfold shining. The golden nature signifies God's essence, the shape signifies Christ as the embodiment of the Triune God, and the seven lamps are the seven Spirits (4:5).

The Trinity is here: the Spirit is shining forth, Christ is the embodiment, and God is the very essence. What is the church? The church is a composition, a constitution, of the Triune God, shining forth God's virtues and attributes in the dark night so that all can see the light. We need message upon message to describe what the church is, but God's wisdom is to show us a lampstand. Saints, this is the church. Look at the church. The lampstand is the church. The church is not muddy but golden. It is of the divine nature of God. It is not without form but shaped. It is not dark but shining. This is the church.

The Seven Stars

The second sign is the seven stars, which accompany the lampstands. The seven stars are the messengers, or angels, of the churches (1:20). In every church there are some brothers who are stars in spirituality. They are shining stars. Daniel 12:3 says that those who turn many to righteousness will shine like stars. In Matthew 13:43 the Lord said that the righteous will shine forth in the coming kingdom like the sun. But the church messengers do not need to wait until the coming age to shine. They are shining right now. I hope that all the elders in the churches are shining stars. When people go to them, they should come into light. A star shines, enlightens, in a time of darkness. By looking at the stars we can learn what kind of persons the leaders in the church should be.

Jasper—the Appearance of God

After John saw the lampstands and the shining stars, he saw a throne in heaven and One sitting on the throne. That One was like a jasper stone in appearance (Rev. 4:2-3). John saw God in the appearance of jasper. Jasper is a beautiful greenish color, signifying fullness of life. The fullness of life is God's appearance. Jasper is also the appearance of the New Jerusalem (21:11), and its entire wall is built of jasper (v. 18). This indicates that the entire city bears the appearance of God, because it is constituted of those who have been transformed into His image.

We should read Revelation 21:11 with 2 Corinthians 3:18: "We all with unveiled face, beholding and reflecting like a mirror the glory of the Lord, are being transformed into the same image from glory to glory." Revelation 21:11 describes the New Jerusalem as "having the glory of God. Her light was like a most precious stone, like a jasper stone, as clear as crystal." The whole city bears God's glory and shines like jasper; this is because the entire composition of the New Jerusalem has been transformed into God's image. The One sitting on the throne, who is God, looks like jasper, and the entire city looks like jasper. This means that Genesis 1:26 has been fulfilled: "Let Us make man in Our image." Man was to be God's expression, and this is fulfilled in the New Jerusalem. The entire New Jerusalem is an image, an expression, of God. God's appearance can be described by one sign, the sign of jasper.

The Lion of the Tribe of Judah

In Revelation 5:5 Jesus Christ is called the Lion of the tribe of Judah. This title signifies Christ as the triumphant King. All living creatures are under Him. None can subdue Him; rather, He subdues everything. The first time I saw a lion in a zoo, I was afraid that the fence was not strong enough to restrict that bold, triumphant creature. Nothing and no one can subdue our Christ.

The Lamb

Christ is not only a Lion but also a Lamb (v. 6). To Satan and all the enemies Christ is a Lion, but to us, the redeemed ones, He is a Lamb. Are you afraid of a lamb? You may be afraid of a lion, but you would feel loving toward a lamb. To us the Lord Jesus is a Lamb, a redeeming Lamb. To think that in eternity on God's throne there will literally be a lamb with four feet and a tail is not the proper way to understand the Bible. I remind you again: Revelation is a book of signs.

The Universal Woman and the Man-child

The universal woman in Revelation 12 is clothed with the sun. On her head there is a crown of twelve stars, and under her feet is the moon (v. 1). Who is this woman? Most fundamental expositors follow the Brethren teaching, which says that this woman signifies Israel, and her man-child signifies Christ. However, after much studying of the Word, we realized from chapter 12 that this woman is composed of two peoples: those who keep the commandments of God and those who bear the testimony of Jesus (v. 17). The people who keep the law are the Jews, Israel. The people who bear the testimony of Jesus are the New Testament believers. Therefore, to say that this woman signifies Israel is only partially true; it leaves aside the New Testament believers.

To say that the man-child born of this woman is Jesus Christ is erroneous. After this man-child is raptured to the throne of God, three and a half years follow. The thousand two hundred and sixty days in 12:6 are three and a half years, which all agree is the period of the great tribulation. Did the great tribulation come right after the Lord's ascension? It has not come yet. This indicates strongly that the man-child here is not the Lord Jesus.

The woman wears a crown of twelve stars on her head. She is clothed with the sun, and the moon is underneath her feet. These indicate three categories among God's redeemed people: the patriarchs, Israel, and the New Testament believers. The patriarchs are represented by the stars, Israel by the moon, and the New Testament believers by the sun. This woman is therefore a composition of all God's redeemed people, including the patriarchs, the other Old Testament believers, and all the New Testament saints.

The man-child is composed of the overcomers of all generations. Through the centuries, among God's people a small number have been martyred. These were the faithful ones. Right before the great tribulation these martyred saints will be resurrected and raptured to the throne of God.

The Great Red Dragon and the Beast

The great red dragon signifies the devil, Satan (vv. 3-4). At the beginning of the next chapter there is a beast coming up out of the sea, the Mediterranean (13:1-2). This is Antichrist. Actually, he is the coming Caesar, the last Caesar of the revived Roman Empire.

The Harvest and the Firstfruits

On this earth God has a harvest. This harvest signifies all

the saints of the New Testament age living on earth near the time of the Lord's return (14:15). From among these living believers will come the firstfruits. There will be some over-comers living among the believers who ripen earlier and become the firstfruits.

Babylon the Great

Babylon the Great signifies the Roman Church. She is called the great harlot (17:1, 5) because of her sinful relation-ships with the rulers of the earth for her profit.

The Wife of the Lamb

The wife of the Lamb, the bride in Revelation 19:7, will be all the overcomers throughout the generations, including those in the Old Testament times, that is, the dead and resur-rected overcomers plus the living overcomers (the firstfruits). They will be His bride in the thousand years (20:4-6). That one day will be the wedding day. A thousand years to the Lord is one day (2 Pet. 3:8). The entire millennium will be a wedding day. On the wedding day the wife is a bride, but after that day she becomes a wife. After the millennium in eternity the bride will be the wife. All the overcomers among God's redeemed people will be His bride.

The New Jerusalem

Now we come to the last sign, the New Jerusalem. The New Jerusalem is the aggregate of all the lampstands. At the beginning of Revelation there are seven lampstands, local lampstands in this age. At the end of Revelation there is an aggregate, a composite lampstand, not the local ones but the eternal one, the universal one. Revelation begins with the lampstands and ends with the lampstand. The lampstands are signs of the churches; the New Jerusalem is also a lamp-stand, the sign of God's dwelling place.

A REVIEW OF THE SIGNS

All these signs are the main scenes on this divine tele-vision screen of Revelation. The telecast begins with seven lampstands, signifying the churches; then follow seven shining stars, signifying the messengers of all the churches; then there is a jasper stone, signifying God's appearance; then a lion and a lamb, both signifying Christ; then a universal woman with twelve stars on her head, the sun clothing her, and the moon underneath her feet; then a red dragon ready to swallow her child; then a man-child brought forth by her and raptured to the throne of God; then a beast coming up out of the Mediterranean Sea; then a harvest on this earth, and out of the harvest the firstfruits; then a great harlot, the great Babylon, terrible, ugly, abhorred; but then, Hallelujah, a beautiful wife, the bride; then finally, something brighter, something greater, the New Jerusalem, which is God's tabernacle just as Jesus was God's tabernacle when He was on earth.

This New Jerusalem is not only a tabernacle to God but also a wife to God's Son, Jesus Christ. God will have a tabernacle, and Christ will have a wife. Both the tabernacle and the wife are the same: the New Jerusalem.

UNDERSTANDING REVELATION

This is the book of Revelation, containing all these crucial signs. If you understand them, you understand the entire book of Revelation. With such a clear and accurate view, do you believe that the New Jerusalem will be a physical city built by God throughout all the centuries? Revelation is a book of signs. Every main item is a sign. Signs should not be interpreted literally. Do you think the church is an actual stand with seven lamps shining? This is a wrong understanding. Do you believe that Jesus Christ is a real lamb? This is ridiculous. Do you believe that the coming Caesar of the Roman Empire will be a real beast that comes up out of the Mediterranean Sea and jumps onto the shore? Do you believe that the wife of the Lamb in Revelation 19 will be a woman adorned with a long wedding gown? Again, it makes no sense to understand it this way.

INTERPRETING THE NEW JERUSALEM

Then how about the New Jerusalem? In the same principle, it does not make sense to think of the coming New Jerusalem as a physical city. Just because this book uses the lion as a sign of Christ as the triumphant King, we should not think that Christ is like a lion in the zoo. The lion is not a real lion—it is a sign of Christ as the triumphant King. The lamb is not a real lamb—it is a sign of Christ as the Redeemer. In the same way, the New Jerusalem is a sign; it signifies something spiritual.

A principle in interpreting the Bible is to be consistent. Since we do not take the other signs literally, we may be sure that the New Jerusalem is not a physical city for us to live in. Such an interpretation is altogether natural. If you do not interpret Christ as a lion with four legs and a tail, why would you think that the New Jerusalem is an actual city? The lion is a sign, and the city is also a sign.

The Key to Revelation

Revelation 1:1 is the key verse to the entire book. Just this one key can open all the doors. We have the master key. We can go to any door and open it. We must pick up 1:1 as the master key. The key point is "by signs." All the pictures in this book are signs.

Fundamental teachers would surely agree that Christ as a lamb does not have four legs and a little tail. They would not make such a ridiculous interpretation. But what about the New Jerusalem? When I was young, I also believed that the New Jerusalem was a heavenly mansion. I was happy in the belief that one day we would be in a mansion. As part of our gospel preaching, we had a song about how we would enter the pearly gates and walk on the golden street. Gradually, however, as I studied the Bible, I found out that the New Jerusalem is a wife. Who would marry a literal city? Even if that city had twelve gates of pearl and a golden street, would anyone marry it?

In studying and understanding the holy Word, Christians often bring in their natural thought. In the new heaven and new earth we will dwell in the New Jerusalem. But we must not think of the New Jerusalem as a physical city. It is God who will be our abode. When I was young, I heard some Bible teachers discussing what we would eat and where the restroom

would be in the "heavenly mansion." How poor it is to bring in
our natural thought!

Today I asked some saints if they are in the church. When
they answered yes, I asked them to show me the church. The
New Testament tells us that the church is God's house, and
that God is abiding in His house; but where is the church? The
church as God's house and as our home is not a physical building but a composition of living believers (1 Pet. 2:5). It is not a
physical, lifeless entity but an organic composition of living
persons. It exists wherever the believers come together. The
church as God's house today is a composition of living persons;
it is a corporate person. This is true in this age, and it will be
true in eternity.

Consistent with the Whole Bible

The thought of God's house is also in the Old Testament.
Moses says in Psalm 90:1, "O Lord, You have been our dwelling place / In all generations."

The Lord Jesus said that if anyone loves Him, His Father and
He will come to him and make an abode with him (John 14:23).
We will be His abode, and He will be our abode. In John 15 the
Lord said, "Abide in Me and I in you" (v. 4). First John 3:24 and
4:16 say that we abide in God and God abides in us.

In this church age we are abiding in God, and God is abiding
in us. Do you believe that when we enter into the new heaven
and new earth we will get out of God and God will get out of us?
If in this age we can dwell in God, taking Him as our dwelling
place, and can give God a place in us, it is not logical to think
that in eternity we will no longer have Him as our dwelling
place but rather live in a golden city as our dwelling place.

We must believe that our abiding in the Lord and His abiding in us will be intensified, enlarged, and uplifted to the
uttermost. This is why John says he saw that the city had no
temple in it, "for the Lord God the Almighty and the Lamb are
its temple" (Rev. 21:22). This is a strong indication that the
city is not a physical place. In this city the temple is a person.
This person is God and the Lamb. The very Triune God will be
the temple. If the temple within the city is a person, do you
believe the city could be something lifeless?

Since the temple is a divine person, the Triune God Himself, the city must be composed of persons also. Actually, the entire city is the Holy of Holies with three equal dimensions (1 Kings 6:20; Rev. 21:16). Since the Triune God will be the temple and the entire city will be the Holy of Holies, the city cannot be something physical. It must be an organic composition.

In New Testament times God's dwelling on this earth was first an individual person, Jesus Christ. He was God's tabernacle. Then following Him, the church is God's temple (Eph. 2:21-22; 1 Cor. 3:16). Jesus, an individual person, was God's tabernacle, His dwelling place. Then the church as a corporate person became the temple of God, God's dwelling. This is the New Testament. After the New Testament age, when we get into eternity, God's dwelling will not change from living persons to a lifeless, physical city. We must believe that these persons built together as God's dwelling place will be enlarged and intensified. In the coming age there will be an enlargement of these living persons as God's dwelling place.

Not a Literal City

If the New Jerusalem were an actual city made of gold, pearls, and precious stones, it would mean that a physical city is the conclusion of the entire divine revelation. This is not logical. God has been working throughout the ages. First He created the universe; then He created man. Afterward, He became incarnate to redeem man. He lived on this earth, was crucified, and then resurrected, ascended, and poured Himself out as the Spirit upon His disciples. The disciples then went out to preach the gospel. Many have been saved and added to the church; they are being built up as a Body to express Christ. Do you believe the final outcome will be that God gains merely a physical city? Do you think that this is God's intention?

If this were the case, God would be a poor architect. Through His creation, incarnation, crucifixion, resurrection, and ascension, through His building up of the churches and the perfecting of the saints in generation after generation, God is preparing something far greater than a big literal city. God has already created something more splendid than a city—the universe. The solar system is beautiful, but God is not satisfied with that. How could He be satisfied with a city, even a city that is half the size of the United States? To interpret such a vision, such a sign, in a natural way is wrong.

The church today is our home. When we come to the church, we come home. The church is in God. The church life with God is everywhere. There are churches in Dallas, Houston, Hong Kong, and all over the earth. Hallelujah! Wherever we go, our home is there. Our home is the church. Why worry about whether we will have a house in the New Jerusalem? We do not need to worry about this. God is not interested in these physical things. This physical thought has to go.

God's Dwelling Place for Eternity

What God cares about is a living composition of His chosen, redeemed, regenerated, transformed, and glorified people. All these will be built together to express God for eternity. This will satisfy God forever. Satan will be in the lake of fire. God will be in His living dwelling place. All those He created, chose, redeemed, regenerated, and transformed will be glorified into His image. He will be living in them, and they will be living in Him. No one can adequately explain such a profound concept. Marvelous! This will be God's dwelling and the wife of His dear Son, Christ. No physical building can be a wife. A wife is something organic, a living person.

The New Jerusalem signifies God's dwelling in the new heaven and new earth. In the New Testament God's dwelling place on earth was first an individual man, Jesus Christ, signified by the tabernacle (John 1:14), and then a corporate man, the church, signified by the temple (1 Cor. 3:16). In the new heaven and new earth, God's dwelling, as the wife of the Lamb (Rev. 21:9-10), is also a living composition of His redeemed people, composed of both the Old Testament saints, represented by the twelve tribes, and the New Testament saints, represented by the twelve apostles (vv. 12, 14).

These people, built together to be God's dwelling, first experienced regeneration through Christ's death and resurrection. This is signified by the pearl gates, their entrance into the city. A pearl is produced by an oyster, a living creature in the death waters. When a grain of sand wounds the oyster, it secretes a substance around the sand, which makes the sand become a pearl. The wound of the oyster signifies death, and the secretion of life-juice around the grain of sand signifies the resurrection life. Jesus' death and resurrection make us pearls through regeneration. No one can enter into the kingdom of God except by regeneration (John 3:5).

In the holy city God's nature, or God's essence, becomes our basic element, signified by gold (Rev. 21:18b, 21b); the city proper is gold, and the street is gold. The essence of all believers is just God Himself.

By the Spirit's work we will be transformed into the image of God, signified by jasper. The Father's nature (gold), the Son's redemption and our regeneration (pearl), and the Spirit's transforming work (precious stones) produce all the components that comprise this eternal dwelling of God. God's dwelling is also our dwelling. We will also be built together to be God's Holy of Holies, expressing Him in glory.

The Last and Greatest Sign

I hope that we will all be impressed with the proper interpretation and understanding of this last and greatest sign in the entire Bible. Of all sixty-six books of the Bible, the New Jerusalem is the last and greatest sign. The last word is the deciding word. God, through creation, incarnation, redemption, resurrection, ascension, and all His transforming, building work through all these Christian centuries, will get a living composition of His redeemed people to be His dwelling and His counterpart to fully satisfy Him. We will join Him because we will be His counterpart.

The Lord Jesus told the Sadducees in Matthew 22:30 that in the resurrection there will be no marriage but that we will all be like the angels. The Bible does not tell us about physical matters or relationships in eternity. What it reveals is high and profound. We must be delivered from our human, natural mentality in considering the New Jerusalem as a physical abode. We must realize what is on God's heart. He needs an eternal dwelling, composed of billions of transformed and glorified living persons, to be His living dwelling place and His dear wife, His counterpart. This ultimate consummation makes it worthwhile for Him to bring creation into existence, to be incarnated, to die on the cross, to be resurrected, and to spend so many centuries to build the churches.

If the New Jerusalem were a literal city, it would be only half the size of the United States (cf. Rev. 21:16). The United States today has a population of about a quarter billion people. Through the generations, though, God will have saved billions of people. How could billions of people live in a city half the size of the United States? We should not follow the natural teachings but rather exercise our sober mind to see what God desires.

The Word is the truth. Thank God He has given us this book. We have something solid in human language that we can study again and again. The Lord Jesus told Peter that He would build His church upon this rock (Matt. 16:18). Peter tells us that we all as living stones are being built up as a spiritual house (1 Pet. 2:5). Paul says that he laid the foundation, but we must all be careful how we build: we must build with gold, silver, and precious stones (1 Cor. 3:10-12). The thought of God's building is throughout the entire New Testament right to the end. This is why we say that the New Jerusalem is the ultimate consummation of God's building work through all the generations.

CHAPTER TEN

THE NEW JERUSALEM—
THE ULTIMATE CONSUMMATION

(3)

Scripture Reading: Rev. 21:2-3, 10-23; 22:1-2a, 14, 17, 19

TWO MAIN SCHOOLS OF INTERPRETATION

The New Jerusalem has been a puzzle to Bible readers and teachers throughout the twenty centuries of the Christian era. There have been two main schools of interpretation. One school says that the New Jerusalem is a physical city; it will be part of the new heaven and new earth and will be on the earth as a literal city. The second school, which is very shallow, says that the New Jerusalem is the heavenly mansion.

However, we should not think of this city as being physical, nor as a heavenly mansion. Let us put aside these different schools, which come from human understanding.

It is very significant that the New Jerusalem stands at the end of God's entire revelation and occupies the final two chapters. We need the whole Bible to understand, interpret, and designate what its meaning is. The conclusion of a book must be the final word concerning its contents. This is a principle. Any book that is meaningful surely has some proper, definite contents and also a proper, definite conclusion. Let us come to the entire Bible from Genesis to Revelation. We must consider its contents and then look at its conclusion.

A REVELATION OF GOD'S DWELLING PLACE

The Bible is a complete revelation of God's dwelling place.

This dwelling place is for Him to rest, to be satisfied, and to be expressed.

Genesis 1:1 says that in the beginning God created the heavens and the earth. Then, after all the things in the universe were created, God made Adam on the sixth day. God wanted to have man. He prepared the heavens, the earth, and everything else for this man whom He made in His own image and according to His likeness.

This is a strong indication that God wanted an expression. He wanted something living and organic to bear His image and to have His likeness. *Image* refers to something inward, whereas *likeness* refers to something outward. Inwardly, we all have the intellect, the will, and the emotion. Outwardly, we have the likeness, the bodily form.

In Genesis 1 we are told that God created the animals according to their kind and the plants according to their kind. The horse, for example, is according to the horse kind, and the peach tree and the apple tree are each according to their kind. *Kind* means "a family, a biological genus." Man, however, was not made according to man's kind. Man was made according to God's kind. We men are of God's kind. We are one family with God because we bear His image and have His likeness. Even though man at this time did not have God's life or His nature, he did have His image and likeness.

This indicates that God wanted an expression. Genesis 1:26-27 shows that man was not just a single person. Verse 27 says, "God created man in His own image;...male and female He created them." This indicates that the man here is something corporate. J. N. Darby says that *man* in Genesis 1:27 means mankind, man as a race. In God's creation He did something according to His plan to have an expression. Mankind was to express God. This is the beginning of the Bible.

Then the Bible goes on to talk about eight great men: Adam, Abel, Enosh, Enoch, Noah, Abraham, Isaac, and Jacob. Including Adam, these are the eight giants in the first book of the Bible.

Bethel—the House of God

When we come to Jacob, without the divine light we can

see only a naughty boy. But this naughty boy, while escaping from his brother Esau, slept in the open air and had a dream (28:11-19).

Jacob dreamed of a ladder set up from earth to heaven, with angels ascending and descending on it. The angels were not descending and ascending but ascending and descending. This indicates that the ladder was from earth to heaven. We usually say that our dreams come from what we think. If we have something on our mind, it will come to us as a dream while we are asleep. In Jacob's case, however, I do not believe that he dreamed what had been in his thoughts during the day. In those days he must have been thinking about how he was running away from Esau. In his dream, though, there was no Esau and no Laban. Jacob saw a ladder reaching from earth to heaven. When he awoke, he had an inspiration from God and said, "This is none other than the house of God, and this is the gate of heaven" (v. 17). He set up the stone that he had used for his pillow and poured oil on it, calling the name of that place Bethel, which means "the house of God."

Noah was commissioned by God to build an ark, and Abraham received a promise from God that the entire earth, all humankind, would be blessed in his seed. But this naughty boy, the grandson of Abraham, had a dream. Waking up from that dream, he said something wonderful, something which composes and directs the entire Bible—the house of God. This is a directing point, running throughout the Bible. Out of this naughty boy who had such a dream came a people, the people of Israel.

The Tabernacle—God's House

In the second book of the Bible, Exodus, all the children of Israel were gained by God. He not only rescued them but gathered them together at Mount Sinai. There God gave them a vision (ch. 19), not just a dream. There is a connection between the vision that Moses received from God on Mount Sinai and Jacob's dream. Jacob in his dream saw something related to God's house, and now his descendants, a people who came out of Jacob, were there at Mount Sinai with the heavens opened to them. One of their representatives, Moses, went up the mountain to stay with God, and God showed him the pattern of His house, a pattern of how to build the tabernacle.

The tabernacle is God's house. First Samuel 3:3 calls the tabernacle the temple of Jehovah; that is to say, it was God's house. The tabernacle as the dwelling place of God was also called the temple, the house of God.

On Mount Sinai Moses saw all the designs, and the children of Israel built a tabernacle according to that pattern. In the last chapter of Exodus the tabernacle was erected, and immediately God's glory descended from the heavens and filled this tabernacle (40:34). This is marvelous! It was even greater than God's creative acts. To create the universe was something general, but for God to have a definite spot on this earth that He could descend upon and enter into in the way of glory was truly marvelous. The physical tabernacle was a type of all the children of Israel as God's dwelling place.

The Tabernacle—Jesus Christ, the God-man

Eventually, that type was fulfilled in the Lord Jesus. When the Lord Jesus came, God came. "In the beginning was the Word, and the Word was with God, and the Word was God," and this Word became flesh (John 1:1, 14). We know that this is Jesus in incarnation. When He came in incarnation, He "tabernacled" (v. 14). This indicates that He Himself as the living tabernacle was the fulfillment of the tabernacle in Exodus 40. Jesus as the tabernacle is not a building but a living, organic person. This One who is the tabernacle is a divine person, a wonderful person, a God-man. The first impression the Bible gives concerning the tabernacle is that it is an organic thing, an organic person. Even more it is an organic human mingled with God. The tabernacle is the God-man, Jesus Christ.

At the end of the Bible is the New Jerusalem, the ultimate consummation of the tabernacle (Rev. 21:3). The tabernacle in the two Testaments, both Old and New, is actually a living person of two natures—the human nature and the divine nature. The Lord Jesus was a man composed of divinity and humanity. The Holy Spirit is the divine element, the divinity, and the human virtue is the human element, humanity.

Therefore, Jesus' conception is of the divine element in the human element. This conception brought forth a child of two natures—divine and human. This child was not only human but also divine. He was a God-man, and this God-man was the tabernacle.

Let me stress strongly that this is a tabernacle in the biblical sense. In the Bible the tabernacle is a living person as a composition of the divine nature and the human nature. Because of this, the New Jerusalem cannot be a literal city, nor can it be a heavenly mansion. According to the biblical sense, *tabernacle* means a living person as a composition of divinity and humanity.

The Tabernacle and the Temple

Israel first built the tabernacle. Then when they entered into the good land, God revealed to them through David (2 Sam. 7:2, 5-13) that He wanted to have something solid and not portable. The tabernacle was a "portable" house of God. It could satisfy God temporarily but not permanently. He wanted something solid built on a solid foundation. The temple was not movable or portable but something settled. David knew God's heart and prepared all the materials for the building of the temple (1 Chron. 22). God had given him a son, Solomon, who would build the temple. This temple was the enlargement of the tabernacle. When it was finished, the things from the tabernacle were brought into the temple (2 Chron. 5:1, 5), indicating that the two were actually one.

In the New Testament the Lord Jesus in John 1:14 is revealed as the tabernacle, but in John 2:19-21 He indicated that He is the temple. "Destroy this temple, and in three days I will raise it up" (v. 19). Jesus' word here indicates that His body was the real temple. He said that He would raise up the temple in three days; He raised up a house of God in resurrection. The house of God that Jesus built up in resurrection is not only Himself but includes His believers also (Eph. 2:6). Thus, this temple built in and by the resurrection of Jesus is a corporate one. This temple is the church. The church is the temple (1 Cor. 3:16).

The Church—
Composed of the Living Members of Christ

Many Christians consider the church to be a physical building. They refer to the building as the church or as the sanctuary. Many think of a church as a building with a steep roof, stained-glass windows, and a bell tower.

The Bible, however, reveals that the church is a living composition of the living members of Christ (1 Pet. 2:5). It is an organic composition of all real believers. We are the church. It is not a lifeless building. The church is organic. The church is we, you and I, the persons regenerated by the Spirit with the divine life. It is all the dear saints. The church is an organism. It is living and alive. It is not lifeless, for the components of the church are living persons. We the believers are the components. The church is composed of all the saints, so it is something living.

The Church—Humanity and Divinity

The church is also a corporate person composed of the two elements of humanity and divinity. We the believers as the components of the church have two natures—a human nature and a divine nature. We received our human nature by our natural birth. Then in our second birth, a spiritual birth, we received another nature, the divine nature. At our regeneration we received the divine life (1 John 5:11). If we have life, surely with that life goes the nature. We are partakers of the divine nature (2 Pet. 1:4); therefore, we have two natures.

There is a trend today among seminary students to believe that Christians have only one nature, which will be gradually improved. This is not only a wrong teaching; it is heretical. Such a teaching annuls the fact of regeneration.

The church, however, is a living, corporate composition of people with two natures—human and divine. With Christ there was divinity first, then humanity. With us there is humanity first, then divinity. Christ as the tabernacle was a person with divinity plus humanity, and we, as the enlargement of Christ, God's dwelling place, the very temple, are a composition of first humanity and then divinity. Christ has divinity plus humanity. We have humanity plus divinity. In nature He and we are the same. The only difference is that He has the Godhead, and we do not; yet we do have the divine life and nature as He does. We do not have His headship, His deity.

The Consummation of the Temple

The New Jerusalem is the consummation of such a temple. Based upon this principle, we cannot say that it is a physical city or a heavenly mansion. Since the New Jerusalem is the ultimate consummation of all the building of God's dwelling through the generations as the conclusion of God's entire revelation of His economy, it is altogether organic. It is human beings mingled with God. This composition will be a mutual abode for God to dwell in the saints and for the saints to dwell in God.

The New Jerusalem is a composition of God's redeemed and regenerated people, who are His sons. This city is also the aggregate of the divine sonship. Ephesians 1 says that we were chosen and predestinated unto sonship (vv. 4-5). The aggregate of sonship will be the New Jerusalem. It is a composition of all God's sons (Rev. 21:7). Such a building, the holy city, is a living corporate person because it is called the wife of the Lamb (v. 9). A physical city cannot be a wife. A wife is a person; therefore, this city should be a living corporate person.

THE INTRINSIC ELEMENTS OF GOD'S BUILDING

The contents of God's building have some elements, which are intrinsic, hidden, and inward. The intrinsic element of the New Jerusalem as God's eternal dwelling place is the Triune God Himself.

The Divine Trinity—the Basic Structure

The Divine Trinity is the basic structure of the New Jerusalem. It is structured with the Father's nature, as signified by gold. The city proper is a mountain of gold, and its street is also gold (vv. 18b, 21b). This indicates that the city is a divine thing. Divinity is the basic element of the contents of the building.

The Son's redemption through death and resurrection is signified by the pearl. Pearls come out of oysters. They are produced after the oysters are wounded by a grain of sand. The oyster secretes its life-juice around the sand and makes it a pearl. This signifies Christ's incarnation and His going into the death waters like an oyster. His being wounded for our transgressions and the releasing of His resurrection life produce a pearl.

The Spirit's transformation is signified by the precious stones. The gold refers to the Father's nature, the pearl refers to the Son's redemption through death and resurrection, and the precious stones refer to the Spirit in His transforming work. This means that the very Triune God is the basic structure of the New Jerusalem. The Trinity is also the basic structure of the church life, which is a miniature of the New Jerusalem. The size is much smaller, but the elements are the same.

The Divine Life—
the Inner Supply and Nourishment

For our physical life we daily need supply and nourishment. This is why we have to eat at least three times a day. The divine life is the inner supply and nourishment to all parts of the New Jerusalem. This is indicated by the water of life flowing out of the divine throne to saturate the entire city (22:1, 17). In the water grows the tree of life, which bears twelve kinds of fruit every month, twelve months yearly, to feed the entire city (vv. 2a, 14, 19). The water of life and the tree of life with the fruit of life do the supplying and nourishing. The whole city lives on these two items.

The Divine Light—
Inward Light and Outward Glory

The Divine Trinity is the basic structure, the divine life is the inner supply and nourishment, and the divine light is the inward light and the outward glory for the expression. God in the Lamb is the lamp as the inward light (21:23). In the New Jerusalem we will not need the sun, the moon, candles, kerosene, or electricity. We will not need God-created light or man-made light, for we will have God Himself, who is the inward light. At the same time this light shines in and through the precious stone, as a jasper stone, signifying the transformed believers (v. 11). The jasper stone is "as clear as crystal." God as the light within the Lamb as the lamp is shining through the city. Within the city is the shining light. Without, the light is expressing God's glory so that the entire city bears the glory of God. The glory of God is God Himself, shining out of the city through the transparent wall of jasper (v. 18). This is what the church should be today—a living composition of God, with Christ as our inner shining light and as our outward expression in glory.

A Mingling of the Triune God with the Tripartite Man

We have been redeemed and regenerated, and now we are being transformed. We are also on the way to being glorified. Our spirit has been regenerated, our troublesome soul is being transformed, and our poor body is awaiting transfiguration.

In the New Jerusalem the Triune God is fully mingled with the redeemed, regenerated, transformed, and glorified tripartite man. This mingling is the eternal dwelling of God, signified by the number twelve. Twelve is three multiplied by four. We know this because the city is square with four sides. On each side are three gates (v. 13). For eternity the New Jerusalem will be an absolute mingling, not just an addition. It is multiplication—the Triune God (three) multiplied by man (four).

In the New Jerusalem the number twelve is used fourteen times. Twelve foundations of twelve precious stones bear the names of the twelve apostles (vv. 14, 19-20). Twelve gates of twelve pearls with twelve angels bear the names of the twelve tribes (vv. 12, 21a). The city's measurement is twelve thousand stadia in three dimensions (v. 16). The height of the wall is one hundred forty-four cubits (v. 17a), which is twelve multiplied by twelve cubits. The tree of life produces twelve fruits in each of the twelve months yearly (22:2). The number twelve, occurring so many times, means that the holy city is a mingling of the Triune God with the tripartite man.

A Building in Resurrection

Revelation 21:17b says the wall's measurement is "the measure of a man, that is, of an angel." This is a sign that by then man will be like the angels. In Matthew 22:30 the Lord Jesus indicated that in resurrection man will be "like angels in heaven." Thus, man's being like an angel indicates the principle of resurrection. The entire city, therefore, will be in resurrection. Christ the Head and we His members will all be in resurrection.

A Full Expression of the Triune God

The wall is made of jasper, and the light of the city is like jasper (Rev. 21:18, 11). In 4:3 we are clearly told that God sitting on the throne looks like jasper. Jasper, then, signifies God's appearance. In eternity the New Jerusalem will bear God's appearance. God looks like jasper, and the entire city will bear the appearance of jasper. This indicates that it will be a corporate and eternal expression of God.

This fulfills Genesis 1:26. The Bible begins the way it ends. It begins with God's image for His expression, and it ends with a corporate, vast, immense, splendid expression. This is the ultimate consummation of the record of the tabernacle and the temple. The Bible is a record of these two things: the tabernacle and the temple. The conclusion of the Bible is the consummation of the tabernacle and the temple.

What the New Jerusalem is should be true of the church right now. We as the church in the Lord's recovery must have the Triune God as our structure, with the divine life as our inner supply and nourishment, and with the divine light as our inward shining and outward expression. This is the testimony of Jesus. At the beginning of the book of Revelation there are the lampstands as the testimony of Jesus (1:2, 12). Then at the end of the same book there is the aggregate of all the lampstands, the New Jerusalem, as the eternal testimony of Jesus. Today we should be such a living testimony of Jesus. We are not another Christian work, nor are we simply

a Christian group. We are the testimony of Jesus as the lampstand today, which will be consummated in the New Jerusalem. What we will be there, we should first be here.

CHAPTER ELEVEN

THE NEW JERUSALEM—
THE ULTIMATE CONSUMMATION

(4)

Scripture Reading: Rev. 21:3-4, 6-7, 24, 26; 22:2-5, 14, 17

The New Jerusalem is the consummation of the entire divine revelation. The sixty-six books of the Bible have a conclusion, and this conclusion is the New Jerusalem. The Bible begins with God's creation and ends with His building. The creation is not God's goal. It is for His goal, which is the building. This thought of the divine building runs through the whole Bible.

THE OLD TESTAMENT

The vision of God's building first came to Jacob. While he was escaping from his brother, Esau, he had a dream. He dreamed about God's house, Bethel (Gen. 28:11-19). Later, God brought Jacob's descendants out of Egypt and over to Mount Sinai, where they stayed for a long time. While they were there, God showed them the heavenly design of a building, the tabernacle, which would be God's dwelling among His people on earth.

After they entered the good land, God wanted them to build the temple. The Old Testament is a history mainly of the tabernacle and the temple. These two are one—the dwelling place of God on this earth among His people. The history of Jacob's descendants is a history of the tabernacle and the temple in the Old Testament. These two were the center, the focus, of the history of God's Old Testament people on this earth.

THE NEW TESTAMENT

In the New Testament we see God incarnated. God became flesh. John 1:14 tells us that this incarnated One "tabernacled among us." John particularly used this word *tabernacled*. It indicates that when the Lord Jesus was on earth in the flesh, He was God's tabernacle. In typology the tabernacle built in Exodus was a full type of the Lord's incarnation; the Lord was incarnated to be the very embodiment of God on this earth. This embodiment was God's dwelling. Colossians 2:9 tells us that the fullness of the Godhead dwells in Christ bodily, in Christ with a human, physical body. The very Christ was the embodiment of God, and this embodiment was the tabernacle of God.

In John 2:19 the Lord told the Jews, "Destroy this temple, and in three days I will raise it up." The Lord Jesus' physical body was a temple of God (v. 21). The tabernacle is in John 1, and the temple is in John 2. The Lord's word *in three days* signifies His resurrection. Paul tells us in Ephesians 2:6 that when Christ was raised, we were resurrected together with Him. Peter says further that through that all-inclusive resurrection we have all been regenerated (1 Pet. 1:3). We have been born of God and are His sons. This implies that the very temple the Lord Jesus built up in three days, that is, in His resurrection, is not an individual thing but a corporate thing. Therefore, in the Epistles we are told that the church as the Body of Christ is God's temple. First Corinthians 3:16 says that the saints are the temple of God.

The New Testament ends with the New Jerusalem, and the New Jerusalem as the conclusion of the Bible is called the tabernacle (Rev. 21:3). John says that he did not see any temple in the holy city, "for the Lord God the Almighty and the Lamb are its temple" (v. 22).

As we have pointed out, the measurement of the New Jerusalem is the same in length, breadth, and height. In three dimensions the city measures twelve thousand stadia (v. 16). The principle revealed in the Bible is that a building with the same three dimensions indicates the Holy of Holies. The Holy of Holies in the tabernacle was ten cubits in three dimensions.

According to 1 Kings 6:20, the Holy of Holies in the temple was also three equal dimensions of twenty cubits each. According to the measurement of the New Jerusalem, then, this holy city must be the Holy of Holies. If we read Revelation 21 carefully, we can see that the holy city is both the tabernacle and the temple.

Both the Old Testament and the New Testament are focused on the tabernacle and the temple as God's dwelling. Then the conclusion of the entire Bible, both the Old Testament and the New Testament, is also the tabernacle and the temple. In the Old Testament the tabernacle typifies Christ individually as God's tabernacle, and the temple typifies Christ corporately as God's temple. What we have here is Christ and the church. Christ is the fulfillment of the type of the tabernacle, and Christ as the Head together with the church as His Body fulfills the type of the temple. This will have a consummation, and this ultimate consummation will be the New Jerusalem, which is both the tabernacle and the temple. Here is the ultimate consummation of God's dwelling, which He has been building for centuries. Further, this New Jerusalem is a living composition of all the saints of the Old Testament, as represented by the names of the twelve tribes, and of all the saints of the New Testament, as represented by the names of the twelve apostles. It is a living composition of God's redeemed people to be His eternal dwelling place.

FOUR DISPENSATIONS FOR GOD'S BUILDING

In the old creation, before the coming of the new heaven and new earth, there are four dispensations. The dispensation of the patriarchs, from Adam to Moses, was the dispensation before law. You may call it the pre-law dispensation or the dispensation of the patriarchs. The second is the dispensation of law, from Moses to Christ's first coming. The third is the dispensation of grace, lasting from Christ's first coming to His second coming. Then with His second coming, the fourth dispensation will begin, that is, the thousand-year reign of Christ. After this fourth dispensation the old creation will surely be entirely renewed because through these dispensations God will have accomplished what He intends to accomplish.

God's creation work was complete in the first two chapters of the Bible. Then from the second half of Genesis 2, God began His building work. This work goes on for all four dispensations: the dispensation of the patriarchs, the dispensation of law, the dispensation of grace, and eventually the dispensation of the thousand-year reign. Through these four dispensations God accomplishes His building.

GOD'S WORK—A WORK OF BUILDING

God's work through all four dispensations is a work of building. In the Old Testament we see the building of the tabernacle and the temple, which was the focus of Old Testament history. When the Lord Jesus came, He was the tabernacle. After helping His disciples to realize that He was the Christ, the Son of the living God, He immediately revealed that He would build His church (Matt. 16:18). The Lord's word indicated that He was doing a building work.

This thought of building is very strong in the Bible. Even in Acts 4 Peter told the Jewish leaders that they were the builders who had rejected Christ, the living stone, yet God had raised Him up and made Him the cornerstone of His building (vv. 10-11). Peter tells us in his writing that the Lord is the living stone, and we all as living stones come to Him and are being built up as a spiritual house (1 Pet. 2:4-6).

Paul also speaks of the building. He tells us that he has laid the unique foundation, and that no one can lay another. The problem, however, is how we build upon the foundation. We can build either with gold, silver, and precious stones or with wood, grass, and stubble (1 Cor. 3:10-12).

In John's writings the thought of building is stronger. When Simon came to the Lord Jesus in John 1:41-42, the Lord changed his name to Cephas, which means "a stone." Later in the same chapter the Lord told Nathanael that he would "see heaven opened and the angels of God ascending and descending on the Son of Man" (v. 51). Actually, the Lord was referring Nathanael to the dream of his forefather Jacob (Gen. 28:12, 17, 19), indicating that a building work of Bethel, the house of

God, was beginning. Then in John 2 the Lord indicated that He would build up His body in resurrection as God's corporate temple (vv. 19, 21-22).

John writes further in Revelation that the overcomers will be made pillars in God's temple (3:12). Eventually, in Revelation 21 he shows us that the ultimate consummation of this building work will be the New Jerusalem, the tabernacle and temple of God, built with gold, pearls, and precious stones and having the apostles as the twelve foundation stones.

Notice, then, that in the entire Bible only one and a half chapters are on God's creation. The rest of the Bible, from the second half of Genesis 2 to the end of Revelation, is on God's building. This building is termed *the tabernacle* and *the temple* again and again in the Old Testament, in the New Testament, and at the conclusion of the Bible. In the Old Testament are the tabernacle and the temple. In the New Testament is the reality of the tabernacle and the temple. At the conclusion of these two Testaments is the ultimate consummation of the tabernacle and the temple.

THE AGGREGATE OF THE DIVINE SONSHIP

This consummation, the New Jerusalem, is the aggregate of the divine sonship for the corporate expression of the Triune God (Rom. 8:23). The Son is the expression of the Father. No one has ever seen God, but the only begotten Son has declared Him (John 1:18). A father and his sons bear one image. The faces of the sons are like the face of the father. Jesus Christ as the Son of God is the very expression of God the Father. God, however, would like to have more than one son. Christ is referred to as the only Begotten in John 1:18 and in John 3:16, where it says that God gave His only begotten Son. From Romans 8:29 we know that in resurrection this unique Son of God became the Firstborn among many brothers. The Lord Jesus in His resurrection charged one of the sisters to "go to My brothers" (John 20:17), and Hebrews 2:11 says that He is "not ashamed to call them brothers," because they were all born of the same Father. The only difference is that He is the first Son, and we are the many sons.

Leading Many Sons into Glory

The Triune God is still working today to bring His many sons into glory (v. 10). We are sons of God, but we are not in glory yet. Just as a caterpillar is transformed into a butterfly, so we are being led into glory. Hallelujah, we are on the way! One day we will all be there in glory as the many sons of God. Romans 8:18-22 tells us that the entire fallen creation, now under the slavery of corruption, eagerly expects to see us in glory. That glory will be the freedom of the glory of the children of God, which is our full redemption (v. 23). Our body has not yet been redeemed, but one day it will be transfigured into a glorious body (Phil. 3:21). This full redemption of our body is the full sonship. Our spirit has already been born of God, but our body has not yet been brought into sonship. The entire universe is eagerly expecting the final part of our redemption. The creation wants to see all the sons of God brought into glory to enjoy their full sonship.

Sons, Brothers, and Members

Before His resurrection Christ was God's only Begotten, but through death and resurrection He became the Firstborn, followed by the many sons who were produced through His death and resurrection. Now to God we are the many sons, to Christ we are the many brothers, and to His Body we are the members. This is why we call ourselves brothers. We are brothers to each other because we are the brothers of Christ and the sons of God. This is sonship. It is a corporate entity.

Total Sonship

The New Jerusalem is the aggregate of the divine sonship. There is only one divine sonship; we are all in this one sonship. In resurrection we will all be males, including the sisters. In this body of the old creation we still have the difference between brothers and sisters, but in resurrection we will all be males, brothers. The total sonship will be completed through the coming rapture and resurrection. When we are there in the New Jerusalem, that will be an aggregate of the divine sonship. This sonship is for the corporate expression of the great God who is triune—the Father, the Son, and the Spirit.

PREDESTINATED UNTO SONSHIP

This sonship fulfills the desire of God's predestination. Ephesians 1:4-5 tells us that before the foundation of the world God predestinated us unto sonship. When I was young, I loved these verses, but I thought that God had predestinated me unto heaven. Then I thought that I was predestinated unto salvation. Many of us may have thought the same thing. Many times when we read the Bible, we read something from our mentality into it. The Bible does not say that God has predestinated us unto heaven or unto salvation. It says that we have been predestinated unto sonship.

God made a firm decision before the foundation of the world to make you a son. Every chosen one is a sinner, even an enemy to God, but God has the redemptive ability to make you, who are a sinner and an enemy of His, one of His sons. This is the wonder of wonders. God has made us, who were His enemies, His sons.

John says that all those who receive Him, that is, believe into His name, are given authority to become children of God (John 1:12). These are born of God. He came to be the tabernacle (v. 14), desiring that we receive Him and thus be born as sons. The intention of the Lord Jesus, the tabernacle, was that we be born as sons to be the components of the coming temple (2:19, 21-22).

SONSHIP IN ROMANS 8

In Romans 8 Paul is strong in this matter of sonship. Romans 8 says, "As many as are led by the Spirit of God, these are sons of God" (v. 14). God has not given us a spirit of slavery but a spirit of sonship (v. 15). His Spirit witnesses with our spirit that we are children of God (v. 16). The entire creation is eagerly expecting this sonship of ours (v. 19). God is now conforming us to the very image of the Firstborn, Christ (v. 29). We are His brothers today but not fully. We are in the process. When we are conformed to the image of the Firstborn, we will be His very expression in a corporate way.

A CORPORATE EXPRESSION OF GOD

In Revelation God sitting on the throne looks like jasper (4:3). Then in 21:18 John tells us that the wall of the city was made of jasper. These two verses tell us that the New Jerusalem will look like God. The city will be a corporate expression of God.

That God will have a corporate expression is also indicated in His creation of man. Before the ages God predestinated us unto sonship. Then He created man in His own image, according to His predestination, with the intention that one day this created man would be His corporate expression. That day is not here yet. When the four dispensations are over—the dispensations of the patriarchs, of the law, of grace, and of the kingdom—God's work of conforming us to the image of the Firstborn will be completed. Then we will be a living corporate entity, bearing the image of God.

The New Jerusalem is the aggregate of all the sons together as a corporate expression. It is a composition of all the dear saints redeemed by God in all the dispensations, both of the Old and of the New Testaments. They together will be the components of this holy city, the aggregate of the divine sonship, expressing God corporately to fulfill His heart's desire, as indicated in His creating man in His own image. Revelation 21 and 22 are the fulfillment of Genesis 1:26—God having a man in His image.

TWO CATEGORIES

In the new heaven and new earth there are two categories of people. One is the many sons, and the other is the peoples. When we are in the New Jerusalem, we will be the sons of God, not the peoples of God.

In Britain there is a royal family. They are not "the people" but the reigning ones. Saints, have you ever considered that you are not among the ordinary people? You are of the royal family. John tells us in Revelation 1:6 that Christ has made us "a kingdom, priests to His God and Father." We are the sons of the almighty God, who is the King of kings. This makes us members, folks, of the royal family. We are not only sons of God but also members of the kingly family.

Revelation 21:3 says, "They will be His peoples." Then 21:7 says, "He who overcomes...will be a son to Me." In 21:24 there are "the nations." The nations will walk by the light of the holy city. We, the sons, the royal family, are the holy city. To God, then, His sons are one category, and His peoples are another.

In London I was taken to see the changing of the guard in front of the gate of Buckingham Palace. Even in the big city of London, there is a "little city" called Buckingham Palace, where the royal family lives. The New Jerusalem will be the heavenly, spiritual, divine, eternal "Buckingham Palace." Around the royal city are the nations.

In the new heaven and the new earth we will not be the peoples, the nations, but the sons. The sons of God in Revelation 21:6-7 are those who have been born of God through regeneration (John 1:12-13; 1 Pet. 1:3, 4, 23; James 1:18). They are built together through transformation (1 Cor. 3:9-12a; Eph. 2:20-22; 1 Pet. 2:4-6; 2 Cor. 3:18; Rom. 12:2; Eph. 4:23-24). They will be glorified in full conformation to be a corporate expression of the Triune God (Rom. 8:29-30; Heb. 2:10; Rev. 21:11). The nations outside the New Jerusalem are not born again, transformed, or glorified. We are different from the nations.

The Sons of God

The category of people who are reborn, transformed, glorified, and conformed will be the components of the New Jerusalem. Today the believers as the members of the Body of Christ are the components of the church, which is both the house of God and the wife of Christ. The church is not a building. It is a living composition of all the living members of Christ. This living composition is an organism. It is not an organization. Where these people are, there is the organism. We are here as this organism, the church. If we move to Miami, this organism will be there in Miami.

These components—the regenerated, transformed, glorified, and conformed sons of God to be both the house of God and the wife of Christ (vv. 3, 9)—in eternity will eat the tree of life and drink the water of life. These will be the two main, substantial, basic enjoyments of the sons of God. Revelation 22:14 promises that we will have the right to eat of the tree of life. In Revelation 22:17 is a call to drink the water of life. These will be our basic enjoyments in the New Jerusalem for eternity.

Then we will serve God and the Lamb as His slaves (v. 3) for eternity. We will also be kings over the nations—the peoples—for eternity; Revelation 22:5 says that we will "reign forever and ever." The believers as sons of God will all be kings. The angels will be serving ones (Heb. 1:13-14), serving us. They are the servants of the royal family, and we will be kings over the nations. This is the kingdom of God in eternity.

The Peoples of God

The peoples of God in Revelation 21 are a remnant of the sheep described in Matthew 25:31-46. When the Lord Jesus comes back, He will sit on His throne of glory in Jerusalem and will gather all the living, different peoples of the nations to Him. They will be classified into sheep and goats, and He will judge them. The goats, who are on His left hand, will go directly to the lake of fire. The sheep, on His right, will inherit the thousand-year kingdom, which God prepared for them from the foundation of the world. We were predestinated unto sonship *before* the foundation of the world, but the millennium was prepared by God for these sheep *from* the foundation. There is a difference.

This judgment will not be at the great white throne (Rev. 20:11), which follows the millennium. It will be at the throne of Christ's glory before the thousand years. The judgment will not be according to the law of Moses or according to the gospel of grace but according to the eternal gospel (14:6-7). Many Christians have never heard of the eternal gospel. It does not include redemption or the forgiveness of sins. It comprises two things: to fear God and to worship Him. This gospel will be preached by an angel at the time of the great tribulation, which will last three and a half years. This is the time when Antichrist will do all that he can to persecute the Jews and the Christians. In Matthew 25, according to the verdict of Christ's judgment, the Jews and the Christians will be treated quite well by the sheep (vv. 34-36). But a great many will follow Antichrist in persecuting the Jews and the Christians. Christ will make His judgment accordingly, and that judgment will be according to the eternal gospel.

The sheep will be transferred into the millennial kingdom to be the peoples, and the overcoming saints will be kings over them (Rev. 20:4, 6). The sheep will be restored to the original state of man as created by God and will be citizens of the millennial kingdom, enjoying the blessing of the restoration (Acts 3:21). Restoration is not regeneration. To be regenerated is to be born again with another life, God's life, but to be restored is to be brought back to the original state of God's creation.

At the end of the thousand years Satan, after being released, will instigate the last rebellion against God (Rev. 20:7-9). Many of the sheep will join Satan's rebellion and will be burned with fire from heaven. The remnant of the sheep will be transferred to the new earth to be the nations (21:24). God will tabernacle with them, the peoples (v. 3). They will be ruled by the sons of God as kings (22:5). To them there will be no more death, sorrow, crying, pain, or curse (21:4; 22:3a). They will be sustained eternally by the leaves of the tree of life (v. 2). We will eat the fruit, but the nations will enjoy the leaves. They will walk by the light of the holy city (21:24a). With their kings they will bring their glory and honor to the city. They will respect the city and regard it as superior.

A FINAL VIEW

The saints throughout all the dispensations who have been redeemed will be the reborn ones, God's sons, belonging to the royal family. They will be kings in eternity. The restored remnant of the unbelievers will be the peoples, the nations, walking in the light of the city and ruled by the saints. Another category of people is the perished ones. The perished unbelievers will be in the lake of fire (v. 8). This gives us a general view of the new heaven and new earth.

ABOUT THE AUTHOR

Witness Lee was born in 1905 in northern China and raised in a Christian family. At age 19 he was fully captured for Christ and immediately consecrated himself to preach the gospel for the rest of his life. Early in his service, he met Watchman Nee, a renowned preacher, teacher, and writer. Witness Lee labored together with Watchman Nee under his direction. In 1934 Watchman Nee entrusted Witness Lee with the responsibility for his publication operation, called the Shanghai Gospel Bookroom.

Prior to the Communist takeover in 1949, Witness Lee was sent by Watchman Nee and his other co-workers to Taiwan to ensure that the things delivered to them by the Lord would not be lost. Watchman Nee instructed Witness Lee to continue the former's publishing operation abroad as the Taiwan Gospel Bookroom, which has been publicly recognized as the publisher of Watchman Nee's works outside China. Witness Lee's work in Taiwan manifested the Lord's abundant blessing. From a mere 350 believers, newly fled from the mainland, the churches in Taiwan grew to 20,000 in five years.

In 1962 Witness Lee felt led of the Lord to come to the United States, and he began to minister in Los Angeles. During his 35 years of service in the U.S., he ministered in weekly meetings and weekend conferences, delivering several thousand spoken messages. Much of his speaking has since been published as over 400 titles. Many of these have been translated into over fourteen languages. He gave his last public conference in February 1997 at the age of 91.

He leaves behind a prolific presentation of the truth in the Bible. His major work, *Life-study of the Bible,* comprises over 25,000 pages of commentary on every book of the Bible from the perspective of the believers' enjoyment and experience of God's divine life in Christ through the Holy Spirit. Witness Lee was the chief editor of a new translation of the New Testament into Chinese called the Recovery Version and directed the translation of the same into English. The Recovery Version also appears in a number of other languages. He provided an extensive body of footnotes, outlines, and spiritual cross references. A radio broadcast of his messages can be heard on Christian radio stations in the United States. In 1965 Witness Lee founded Living Stream Ministry, a non-profit corporation, located in Anaheim, California, which officially presents his and Watchman Nee's ministry.

Witness Lee's ministry emphasizes the experience of Christ as life and the practical oneness of the believers as the Body of Christ. Stressing the importance of attending to both these matters, he led the churches under his care to grow in Christian life and function. He was unbending in his conviction that God's goal is not narrow sectarianism but the Body of Christ. In time, believers began to meet simply as the church in their localities in response to this conviction. In recent years a number of new churches have been raised up in Russia and in many European countries.

OTHER BOOKS PUBLISHED BY
Living Stream Ministry

Titles by Witness Lee:

Abraham—Called by God	978-0-7363-0359-0
The Experience of Life	978-0-87083-417-2
The Knowledge of Life	978-0-87083-419-6
The Tree of Life	978-0-87083-300-7
The Economy of God	978-0-87083-415-8
The Divine Economy	978-0-87083-268-0
God's New Testament Economy	978-0-87083-199-7
The World Situation and God's Move	978-0-87083-092-1
Christ vs. Religion	978-0-87083-010-5
The All-inclusive Christ	978-0-87083-020-4
Gospel Outlines	978-0-87083-039-6
Character	978-0-87083-322-9
The Secret of Experiencing Christ	978-0-87083-227-7
The Life and Way for the Practice of the Church Life	978-0-87083-785-2
The Basic Revelation in the Holy Scriptures	978-0-87083-105-8
The Crucial Revelation of Life in the Scriptures	978-0-87083-372-4
The Spirit with Our Spirit	978-0-87083-798-2
Christ as the Reality	978-0-87083-047-1
The Central Line of the Divine Revelation	978-0-87083-960-3
The Full Knowledge of the Word of God	978-0-87083-289-5
Watchman Nee—A Seer of the Divine Revelation ...	978-0-87083-625-1

Titles by Watchman Nee:

How to Study the Bible	978-0-7363-0407-8
God's Overcomers	978-0-7363-0433-7
The New Covenant	978-0-7363-0088-9
The Spiritual Man • 3 volumes	978-0-7363-0269-2
Authority and Submission	978-0-7363-0185-5
The Overcoming Life	978-1-57593-817-2
The Glorious Church	978-0-87083-745-6
The Prayer Ministry of the Church	978-0-87083-860-6
The Breaking of the Outer Man and the Release ...	978-1-57593-955-1
The Mystery of Christ	978-1-57593-954-4
The God of Abraham, Isaac, and Jacob	978-0-87083-932-0
The Song of Songs	978-0-87083-872-9
The Gospel of God • 2 volumes	978-1-57593-953-7
The Normal Christian Church Life	978-0-87083-027-3
The Character of the Lord's Worker	978-1-57593-322-1
The Normal Christian Faith	978-0-87083-748-7
Watchman Nee's Testimony	978-0-87083-051-8

Available at
Christian bookstores, or contact Living Stream Ministry
2431 W. La Palma Ave. • Anaheim, CA 92801
1-800-549-5164 • www.livingstream.com